Language Arts Activities for Elementary Schools

Language Arts Activities for Elementary Schools

Paul C. Burns   University of Tennessee

Randall K. Bassett   John Brown University

Houghton Mifflin Company   Boston

Dallas   Geneva, Illinois   Hopewell, New Jersey   Palo Alto   London

"Spelling" by Ernest A. Horn reprinted by permission of Macmillan Publishing Co., Inc., from *Encyclopedia of Educational Research*, 3d ed., Chester W. Harris, ed., page 1345. © American Educational Research Association, 1960.

Printed in the U.S.A.
Library of Congress Catalog Card Number:81-82574
ISBN: 0-395-31688-x

Contents

8 Spelling

9 Handwriting

Preface

PURPOSE

Language Arts Activities for Elementary Schools is intended both for students in undergraduate and graduate language arts methods courses and for inservice language arts teachers in elementary schools. The activities presented here have been designed equally for use in practice teaching sessions and in actual day-to-day teaching.

ORGANIZATION

This text is organized developmentally. Each chapter focuses on a single topic. The topics build sequentially throughout the book—beginning with language, progressing through listening, speaking, writing, vocabulary, and concluding with the integration of language arts into other areas of the curriculum.

The chapters contain brief introductions to the particular topic and, of course, activities related to the topic. The activities themselves are presented as detailed instructions and provide designations of the intended grade level, a statement of the objective of the activity, a list of the materials that will be needed, and an outline of specific directions for implementing the activity; in many cases diagrams show how to use the activity, and variations are listed so as to make the activity easily adaptable to teachers' needs.

GUIDELINES FOR THE ACTIVITIES

In designing the activities in this volume we have followed these guidelines.

1. Each activity develops or reinforces important instructional objectives.
2. Many of the activities can be performed by several students without teacher direction beyond the basic instructions.

3. To help reduce demands on the teacher's time and to provide immediate feedback, self-correction features are incorporated in many activities.

4. Each activity
   a. creates a learning situation that will facilitate skill or concept acquisition;
   b. rewards students for cooperation;
   c. provides an opportunity for students to serve as models for each other;
   d. involves a self-motivating strategy that can extend learning beyond the immediate lesson;
   e. involves the students as actively as possible.

As we explain in Chapter 1, we have also designed this volume to allow for a large measure of *flexibility* in implementation. We encourage teachers to modify these activities so that they may fully meet the needs of their students.

FEATURES

In addition to a detailed table of contents we have included a *subject-skills index*, which will aid the user in locating activities pertinent to chosen topics.

Also included are three *appendixes*: Appendix A lists multilevel language arts instructional materials; Appendix B lists free and inexpensive teaching materials; and Appendix C provides a directory of publisher's addresses.

Frequently, bibliographies of suggested readings and helpful sources also appear with the activities.

ACKNOWLEDGEMENTS

The authors wish to acknowledge their appreciation to the following colleagues who reviewed the original manuscript and contributed to its final shape: Connie Bridge of the University of Kentucky, Leonard Bergquist of Moorhead State University, and Jack Mooers of San Diego State University.

Paul C. Burns
University of Tennessee

Randall K. Bassett
John Brown University

1 Introduction

The activities presented in this text have been designed in accordance with current authoritative theories on the most significant aspects of an elementary school language arts program. These activities will enrich and extend your present curriculum and will provide enjoyable experiences in the language arts. Designed to allow teacher flexibility in implementation and modification, the activities can be used to introduce new concepts, to facilitate the acquisition of new skills and to increase readiness, as well as to sharpen already acquired skills and refresh learned material.

While you can select activities from throughout the text to meet your individual needs, this volume has been organized developmentally. Chapters 2 and 3 introduce and discuss language and language structure; Chapter 4 explores pre- and early school language arts; Chapters 5 and 6 focus on listening and speaking; Chapter 7 deals with written composition, and Chapters 8 and 9 present the mechanics of composition, spelling, and handwriting; Chapter 10 presents vocabulary development; and Chapters 11 and 12 draw on all the previous skills to provide ways to increase the appreciation of language and ways to integrate the activities into other curriculum areas. Throughout the book, literature and reading activities interweave with and augment more directly skill-related activities.

Each chapter begins with an introductory section which explains the relevant area and how the activities relate to the topic. Each activity (numbered for ease of reference and designated for the appropriate level: primary—1–4; intermediate—5–8) begins with a statement of its *Objective*—either what the student will learn (say, familiarity with technical language) or the pedagogical purpose of the activity (say, to introduce a new concept). The *Materials* necessary for the activity are then described, frequently accompanied by a diagram of their use. *Directions* then detail the procedures for carrying out the activity. Often accompanying *Variations* suggest alternative methods and purposes. Many of the activities use and build on such standard teacher-made and collected materials as story and word file cards, contract cards, listening centers, and the instructional bulletin board.

USING LANGUAGE ARTS ACTIVITIES

Success with the activities in this book depends on familiarity with the activities and an accurate assessment of the needs and strengths of your students. As you observe your students at work, note the areas and skills which need development and the students' particular strengths or evidences of readiness. Check the activities to ascertain those which can meet student needs by drawing on the skills they already possess. In using an activity, be sure to let students know how that activity will help.

The activities may be implemented in a number of ways.

1. When new skills are introduced, it will be most effective for the entire class to be involved in that particular activity. Smaller, more manageable groups can, of course, be organized, each group being involved in the same activity.
2. When diagnostic tests indicate a variation in the skill levels among class members, the "neediest" can be engaged in skill acquisition and refinement activities while those who have few difficulties can be involved in enrichment activities.
3. When particular students need practice beyond what can be accomplished during school time, activities can be modified so that they can be used outside of school with family or friends.
4. When in the other content areas student interest needs reviving or particular components need concentrated work, the language arts activities presented here (see Chapter 12, especially) can be integrated into the ongoing curriculum. These activities can provide an enjoyable way to learn difficult material.

The most important thing to remember in using any of the activities is that they should fit the students and not the other way around. We have designed these activities to allow for a great deal of teacher flexibility; they can and should be modified to meet the particular needs of your class. We would point out by way of example that some activities are either competitive or lend themselves to competition. Although many students thrive on the motivational effects of competition, a great many others are adversely affected in trying to learn in a win or lose situation.

Not only can such situations seriously damage a student's self-image, but moreover, the very objective of all the activities—learning—can be defeated. Thus, competition should be used with great care. Far better to create situations in which students cooperate in achieving the objective or compete against their own previous achievements rather than against each other. Based on your assessment, then, you can modify the activities presented here in accordance with your students' reactions to competitive situations.

SOURCES OF LANGUAGE ARTS ACTIVITIES

The following bibliography provides other sources of activities for elementary school language arts programs.

Ashley, Rosalind. *Successful Techniques for Teaching Elementary Language Arts*. West Nyack, NY: Parker Publishing Company, 1970.

Bergman, Floyd. *The English Teacher's Activities Handbook*. Boston: Allyn and Bacon, 1976.

Carlson, Ruth Kearney. *Speaking Activities Through the Grades*. New York: Teachers College Press, 1975.

Carson, Patti, and Janet Dellosa. *Cartloads of Creative Story Starters*. Akron, OH: Carson and Dellosa, 1978.

Carson, Patti; Janet Dellosa; and Sandra Kay Hausfeld. *Ahoy! Sailing to Treasures Through Words*. Akron, OH: Carson and Dellosa, 1978.

Chappel, Bernice M. *Listening and Learning: Practical Activities for Developing Listening Skills*. Belmont, CA: Fearon-Pitman Publishers, 1973.

Cheyney, Arnold. *The Writing Corner*. Santa Monica, CA: Goodyear Publishing Company, 1978.

Crofts, Doreen, and Robert D. Hess. *An Activities Handbook for Teachers of Young Children*, 3d. ed. Boston: Houghton Mifflin, 1980.

Farnette, Cherrie; and others. *Special Kids' Stuff: High Interest, Low Vocabulary Reading and Language Skills Activities*. Nashville, TN: Incentive Publications, 1976.

Forte, Imogene, and Mary Ann Pangle. *Spelling Magic*. Nashville, TN: Incentive Publications, 1976.

Forte, Imogene; Mary Ann Pangle; and Robbie Tupa. *Cornering Creative Writing*. Nashville, TN: Incentive Publications, Inc., 1974.

Gerbrandt, Gary L. *An Idea Book for Acting Out and Writing Language, K–8.* Urbana, IL: National Council of Teachers of English, 1974.

Grant, Neils. *Word Games.* Belmont, CA: Fearon-Pitman Publishers, 1971.

Greff, Kasper, and Eunice N. Askov. *Learning Centers: An Idea Book for Reading and Language Arts.* Dubuque, IA: Kendall/Hunt Publishing Company, 1974.

Grimm, Gary, and Don Mitchell. *The Good Apple Spelling Book.* Carthage, IL: Good Apple, Inc., 1976.

Hendricks, William. *Scribe.* Stevensville, MI: Educational Service, Inc., 1976.

Hennings, Dorothy Grant. *Smiles, Nods, and Pauses: Activities to Enrich Children's Communication Skills.* New York: Citation Press, 1977.

Holden, Margaret M. *Fun with Language Arts.* Dansville, NY: Instructor Curriculum Materials, 1973.

Hucklesby, Sylvia. *Opening Up the Classroom: A Walk Around the School.* ERIC, Clearinghouse on Early Childhood Education (University of Illinois at Urbana), 1971.

Kaplan, Phyllis; Joyce Kohfeldy; and Kim Sturla. *It's Postively Fun.* Denver, CO: Love Publishing Company, 1974.

Kaplan, Sandra; and others. *The Big Book of Writing.* Pacific Palisades, CA: Goodyear Publishing Company, 1975.

Learning Magazine, Editors. *Mud Puddles, Rainbows and Asparagus Tips: Learning's Best Language Arts Ideas.* Palo Alto, CA: Education Today Company, 1979.

Lloyd, Dorothy M. *100 Activities for Classroom Learning Centers.* Dansville, NY: Instructor Curriculum Materials, 1974.

Lorton, Mary Baratta. *Workjobs: Activity Centered Learning for Early Childhood Education.* Reading, MA: Addison-Wesley, 1972.

Lutz, Jack. *Expanding Spelling Skills.* Dansville, NY: Instructor Curriculum Materials, 1973.

Miller, Robert D. *Spelling Games and Puzzles for Junior High.* Belmont, CA: Fearon-Pitman Publishers, 1976.

Moore, Alma, and John E. Pate. *Handbook of Kindergarten Activities.* New York: Teachers Publishing Corporation, 1971.

Muncy, Patricia Tyler. *Word Puzzles.* Belmont, CA: Fearon-Pitman Publishers, 1974.

Norton, Donna. *Language Arts Activities for Children.* Columbus, OH: Charles E. Merrill, 1980.

Phillips, Ward H., and John H. O'Lague. *Successful Bulletin Boards.* Dansville, NY: Instructor Curriculum Materials, 1973.

Platts, Mary E. *Spice*. Stevensville, MI: Educational Service, Inc., 1973.

Polon, Linda, and Aileen Cantwell. *Making Kids Click: Reading and Language Arts Activities*. Santa Monica, CA: Goodyear Publishing Company, 1978.

Reeks, Angela, and James Laffey. *Pathways to Imagination: Language Arts Learning Centers and Activities*. Santa Monica, CA: Goodyear Publishing Company, 1979.

Russell, David H., and Elizabeth Russell. *Listening Aids Through the Grades*, rev. ed. New York: Teachers College Press, Columbia University, 1979.

Saludis, Anthony J. *Language Arts Activities*, 2d. ed. Dubuque, IA: Kendall/Hunt Publishing Company, 1977.

Schaff, Joanne. *The Language Arts Idea Book: Classroom Activities for Children*. Pacific Palisades, CA: Goodyear Publishing Company, 1976.

Scott, Louise Binder; Marion E. May; and Mildred S. Shaw. *Puppets for all Grades*. Dansville, NY: Instructor Curriculum Materials, 1972.

Scoy, Kareny Van, and Robert Whitehead. *Literature Games*. Belmont, CA: Fearon-Pitman Publishers, 1971.

Smith, Charlene W. *The Listening Activity Book: Teaching Literal, Evaluative, Critical Listening in the Elementary School*. Belmont, CA: Fearon-Pitman Publishers, 1975.

Spencer, Zana A. *FLAIR: A Handbook of Creative Writing Techniques for the Elementary School Teacher*. Stevensville, MI: Educational Services, 1972.

Thompson, Richard. *Treasure of Teaching Activities for Elementary Language Arts*. Englewood-Cliffs, NJ: Prentice-Hall, 1975.

Thoop, Sara. *Language Arts for the Young Child*. Belmont, CA: Fearon-Pitman Publishers, 1974.

Tiedt, Sidney, and Iris M. Tiedt. *Language Arts Activities for the Classroom*. Boston, MA: Allyn and Bacon, 1978.

Wade, Priscilla, and Verl Short. *Who Says an Old Lemon Can't Have a New Twist?* Santa Monica, CA: Goodyear Publishing Company, 1979.

SOURCES OF READING ACTIVITIES

This text does not provide activities directly focusing upon reading content and skills since there are a number of reading activity books. The following lists books which provide activities for elementary school reading programs.

Bielawski, J.G., and L. Ponerleau. *Reading Games Make Reading Fun: Reading Games for K-Grade 6.* Georgetown, CT: R.D. Communications, 1973.

Bloomer, Richard H. *Skill Games to Teach Reading.* Dansville, NY: The Instructor Publications, 1973.

Burie, Audrey, and Mary Ann Heltshe. *Reading with a Smile: 90 Reading Games that Work.* Washington, DC: Acropolis Books, 1975.

Burmeister, Lou E. *Words—from Print to Meaning; Classroom Activities: for Building Sight Vocabulary, for Using Context Clues, Morphology, and Phonics.* Reading, MA: Addison-Wesley, 1975.

Criscuolo, Nicholas P. *100 Individualized Activities for Reading.* Belmont, CA: Fearon-Pitman Publishers, 1974.

———. *125 Motivators for Reading.* Belmont, CA: Fearon-Pitman Publishers, 1977.

Croft, Doreen J., and Robert D. Hess. *An Activities Handbook for Teachers of Young Children,* 3d. ed. Boston: Houghton Mifflin, 1980.

Dellosa, Janet, and Patti Carson. *Racing into Reading Skills.* Akron, OH: Carson and Dellosa, 1978.

Dorsey, Mary E. *Reading Games and Activities.* Belmont, CA: Lear Siegler, 1972.

Farnette, Cherrie; Imogene Forte; and Barbara Loss. *Kids' Stuff, Reading and Writing Readiness.* Nashville, TN: Incentive Publications, Inc., 1976.

———; ———; ———. *Special Kids' Stuff.* Nashville, TN: Incentive Publications, Inc., 1976.

Forgan, Harry W. *Phorgan's Phonics.* Santa Monica, CA: Goodyear Publishing Company, 1978.

———. *The Reading Corner.* Santa Monica, CA: Goodyear Publishing Company, 1976.

Forte, Imogene; and others. *Pumpkins, Pinwheels, and Peppermint Packages.* Nashville, TN: Incentive Publications, Inc., 1974.

Forte, Imogene, and Joy MacKenzie. *Kids' Stuff, Reading and Language Experiences—Primary Level.* Nashville, TN: Incentive Publications, Inc., 1974.

Forte, Imogene, and Mary Ann Pangle. *Comprehension Magic.* Nashville, TN: Incentive Publications, Inc., 1977.

Garrison, Evangeline L. *Individualized Reading—Self Paced Activities.* Dansville, NY: The Instructor Publications, 1972.

Gould, Annabelle, and Warren Schollaert. *Reading Activities for Primary and Intermediate Grades*. Dansville, NY: The Instructor Publications, 1972.

Greater San Diego Reading Association. *Reading Games Unlimited,* rev. ed. San Diego, CA, 1974.

Gutzler, Dorothy, and Helen Linn. *110 Reading Comprehension Activities*. Dansville, NY: The Instructor Publications, 1976.

Hall, Nancy A. *Rescue: Remedial Reading*. Stevensville, MI: Educational Services, 1972.

Herr, Selma E. *Learning Activities for Reading*. 3d. ed. Dubuque, IA: William C. Brown, 1976.

Howard, Elizabeth, and Frances Martini. *The Reading Roost*. Santa Monica, CA: The Learning Works, 1977.

Kaplan, Jo Ann; and others. *Change for Children*. Englewood Cliff, NJ: Prentice-Hall, 1972.

Keith, Joy L. *Comprehension Joy*. Naperville, IL: Reading Joy, Inc., 1974.

_____. *Readiness Joy*. Naperville, IL: Reading Joy, Inc., 1975.

_____. *Word Attack Joy.* Naperville, IL: Reading Joy, Inc., 1974.

Kindig, Dean. *Ready! Set! Read!* Dansville, NY: The Instructor Publications, 1978.

Levin, Joyce, and Walter B. Barbe. eds. *Classroom Activities for Encouraging Reluctant Readers*. New York: Center for Applied Research in Education, 1975.

Lorton, Mary Baratta. *Workjobs: Activity Centered Learning for Early Childhood Education.* Reading, MA: Addison-Wesley, 1972.

Love, Marla. *20 Reading Comprehension Games*. Palo Alto, CA: Fearon-Pitman Publishers, 1975.

Mallett, Jerry J. *Classroom Reading Games Activities Kit*. New York: Center for Applied Research in Education, 1975.

_____. *Make-and-Play Reading Games for the Intermediate Grades.* West Nyack, NY: Center for Applied Research in Education, 1975.

Mattleman, M. *101 Activities for Teaching Reading*. Portland, ME: Weston Walch, 1973.

Metzner, Seymour. *77 Games for Reading Groups*. Palo Alto, CA: Fearon-Pitman Publishers, 1973.

Miller, Harry B. *Teacher's Programmed Educational Techniques in Reading (PET)*. Memphis, TN: Al Graci Educational Services, 1974.

Piercey, Dorothy. *Reading Activities in Content Areas*. Boston: Allyn and Bacon, 1976.

Russell, David, and Eta Karp. *Reading Aids Through the Grades: 300 Developmental Reading Activities*, rev. ed. New York: Teachers College Press, Columbia University, 1975.

Schubert, D. *Reading Games that Teach: Comprehension.* Monterey, CA: Creative Teaching Press, 1971.

Sciara, Frank J., and Richard B. Walter. *Reading Activities with the Tape Recorder*. Dansville, NY: The Instructor Publications, 1973.

Senini, Megan L. *Contemporary Fun and Games with Reading.* Englewood Cliffs, NJ: Prentice Hall, 1975.

Shankman, Florence. *Games and Activities to Reinforce Reading Skills*. NY: MSSInformation Corporation, 1972.

Spache, Evelyn B. *Reading Activities for Child Involvement*, 2d. ed. Boston: Allyn and Bacon, 1976.

Thompson, Richard. *Energizers for Reading Instruction*. Englewood Cliffs, NJ: Prentice-Hall. 1973.

Tiedt, Iris M. *Exciting Reading Activities*. San Jose, CA: Contemporary Press, 1975.

Wagner, Guy, and M. Hosier. *Reading Games: Strengthening Reading Skills with Instructional Games*. New York: Teachers Publishing Corp., 1972.

2 Language Study

Certain aspects of language can profitably be used for study as students mature and express an interest in language itself. At appropriate times, therefore, teachers should provide accurate information about language so that students may come to understand its system and how it operates.

The following topics can usefully be included in students' study of language at the elementary school level.

1. Nonverbal language
2. Language characteristics
3. Language structure
4. Language history

This chapter involves specific examples of these four major language topics. These activities should be presented as concepts to be explored and not as skills to be mastered.

NONVERBAL LANGUAGE

The first part presents the idea of nonverbal language (communication without words). The specific activity provides signs to be interpreted: for example, a rural mailbox with the flag up (meaning to "collect mail"). Other variations that illustrate the nonverbal aspect of language could include the examination of pictures and photographs for facial expressions of emotion. Situations may be pantomimed to illustrate further that a message can be sent without using words. Such activities are helpful in pointing out various ways of communicating and the role of words as an effective means of communication.

LANGUAGE CHARACTERISTICS

The activities in the second part of this chapter involve concepts associated with the following language characteristics.

1. *There is a system to language*. One facet of this system is the meaningful arrangement of words in sentences. For example, "ran street down the yesterday girl the" is not meaningful until the order of words reads "Yesterday, the girl ran down the street."

2. *The relation of words to the objects they represent is arbitrary*. People have designated a word or set of words to represent something about which they wish to talk. The Americans say *cat*, the French say *chat*, and the Germans say *Katze*. The cat is the same all over, only the word for cat differs.

3. *Language changes*. Old words may be given new meanings, or new words may be coined from parts of old words to represent new meanings or modifications of old ones. Few of us use words like *fetch* or *tuffet*, except in reading Mother Goose rhymes; and there you will not find such words as *television* and *supersonic*. Additionally, there have been changes in pronunciation and spelling.

4. *There is variety in language*. For example,

Pronunciation: In eastern New England the /r/ in *park* or *father* is often unpronounced, and the intrusive /r/ is common, as in *idea* (r).

Vocabulary: *Clabber cheese* to some in the South is *pot cheese* to those in the Hudson Valley.

Syntax: "Throw the horse over the fence some hay" may be heard in Pennsylvania Dutch country.

Such differences are referred to as "dialects," generally reflecting the geographic area and the socioeconomic status of the speaker. Students need to appreciate the idea that dialects represent differences, not "deficiencies."

LANGUAGE STRUCTURE

The third part of this chapter presents activities which focus upon other features common to the English language system: (a) suprasegmental phonemes; (b) homophones; (c) words composed of Latin and Greek roots and prefixes; and (d) figurative and idiomatic expressions. The first activity introduces the idea that change in the stress on different words within a sentence produces different meanings. English language contains a number of homophones—words that are pronounced the same but spelled differently and possess different meanings (for example, *know* and *no*). Another activity shows that the meaning of some words can be revealed by examining roots and prefixes. The final activity focuses upon figurative expressions. Each activity reveals some insight into the make-up of the language as well as suggests ways to draw attention to sentence and word meaning.

LANGUAGE HISTORY

The final set of activities in this chapter focuses upon historical aspects of language: (a) the use of hieroglyphics prior to the development of the alphabet; (b) historical origins of words and changes in meanings; and (c) one way in which words are formed— portmanteau words. Such explicit information helps the student to focus on language instead of merely taking it "for granted." From a growing appreciation of language, students can become intrigued with the beauty and richness of the English language.

There are a number of trade or library books that can be used to teach more about language. Such books may be used by individuals or by an entire class for a free-reading experience. Several lists of such books are available.[1] The following is a sample list.

Alphabet: Dugas, William. *How Our Alphabet Grew*. New York: Golden, 1972.

Antonyms: Hanson, Joan. *Still More Antonyms*. New York: Lerner, 1976.

Clichés and *Idioms*: Funk, Charles. *Heavens to Betsy*. New York: Warner, 1972.

Content Area Words: Asimov, Isaac. *Words of Science*. Boston: Houghton Mifflin, 1961.

Dictionary: Rosenbloom, Joseph. *Daffy Dictionary: Funabridged Definitions; From Aardvark to Zuider Zee*. New York: Sterling, 1977.

Foreign Language: Feelings, Muriel. *Swahili Counting Book*. New York: Dial, 1973.

Handwriting: Scott, Joseph, and Lenore Scott. *Hieroglyphs for Fun*. New York: Van Nostrand Reinhold, 1974.

History of Books: Bartlett, Susan. *Libraries: A Book to Begin On*. New York: Holt, Rinehart, 1964.

History of the English Language: Sparke, William. *Story of the English Language*. New York: Abelard-Schuman, 1965.

History of Writing: Cahn, William, and Rhonda Cahn. *The Story of Writing from Cave Art to Computer*. New York: Harvey House, 1963.

---

[1] Paul C. Burns, "Elementary School Language Arts Library—A Selected Bibliography," *Elementary English* 41 (December 1964): 870–884; Maxine Delmare, "Language Books for the Library," *Elementary English* 45 (January 1968): 55–66; Iris M. Tiedt and Sidney W. Tiedt, "A Linguistic Library for Students," in *Contemporary English in the Elementary School*, 2d ed. (Englewood Cliffs, New Jersey: Prentice-Hall, 1975), pp. 44–48; and Ruth M. Noyce and Flora R. Wyatt, "Children's Books for Language Exploration," *Language Arts* 55 (March 1978): 297–301, 357.

Homophones: Hanson, Joan. *Homographic Homophones*. New York: Lerner, 1973.

Language Sounds: Curtis, Foley. *The Little Book of Big Tongue Twisters*. New York: Harvey, 1977.

Nonverbal Language: Rinhoff, Barbara. *Red Light Says Stop!* New York: Lothrop, Lee and Shepard, 1974.

Printing: Epstein, Sam, and Beryl Epstein. *The First Book of Printing*. New York: Watts, 1973.

Word Origins: Hudson, P. *Words to the Wise*. New York: Scholastic Book Services, 1967.

Word Play: Nurnberg, Maxwell. *Fun with Words*. Englewood Cliffs, NJ: Prentice-Hall, 1970.

NONVERBAL

Communicating Without Words

2.1 Nonverbal Messages (Primary)

Objective: To introduce and examine the idea that communication can take place without words.

Materials: A chart with illustrations of suggested ideas.

a rural mailbox with flag up
a railroad crossing with lights flashing
nodding your head
a red light
waving your hand at someone
a green light

Directions: Answer cards should be prepared in advance. Players take turns picking up individual answer cards and placing them beneath the appropriate picture. Answer cards for suggested pictures are: "Mail to Pick Up"; "Do Not Cross"; "Hello"; "Agreeing or disagreeing with Someone"; "Go."

Variations:
1. The answer cards could be posted; the task would then be to match the appropriate pictures.
2. Pantomiming a situation can also show that a message can be conveyed without oral language. Some examples that

might be mimed by an individual or small group for others to decode include:

Hunger—It has been a long time since John last ate. He is very hungry. Because of his hunger, he is nervous and on edge.
Fear—Jan is in a place that she has never visited before. It is dark and cold. She is frightened and her actions show it.
Boredom—Eric has been in class for over an hour. The teacher is reviewing material that Eric knows well. He becomes bored and tries to stay awake.

3. See Activity 11.4 for another nonverbal activity.
4. For many nonverbal activities, see Dorothy Hennings' *Smiles, Nods, and Pauses* (New York: Citation Press, 1974).

LANGUAGE CHARACTERISTICS

Language Is Systematic

2.2 Make a Sentence (Primary)

Objective: To introduce the concept of the system of language by showing the importance of word order to sentence sense.

Materials: Sets of individual 4" × 5" cards as suggested below.

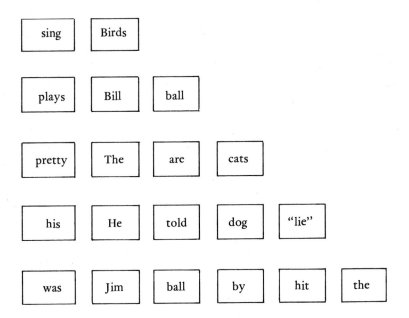

Directions: Prepare cards for two-, three-, four-, five-, or more word sentences. Put the cards for each sentence in a large envelope; one envelope per sentence. Teams of two would be utilized for two-word sentences; three would be used for three-word sentences; and so on. Competing teams each select an envelope containing the same length of sentences. The students are instructed to make a sentence out of the words by standing in position with the word before them. The first team to make a sentence is declared the winning team.

Variations:

1. If this activity is too difficult for some children, a preparatory activity can involve connecting "larger chunks" of sentences together:

2. By increasing the number and level of words in the sentence the activity can be increased in difficulty.

The Relation of Words to Objects Is Arbitrary

2.3 Find the Word Partner (Intermediate)

Objective: To show the arbitrary relationship of words and objects by matching British and American words.

Materials: Construction paper or poster board, pen or marker, and scissors.

Directions: Cut egg shapes out of the construction paper or poster board. Cut a zig-zag line through each egg to "crack" it. Put equivalent British and American words on the egg halves. Mix up the egg halves and instruct the students to match them correctly. Terms might include:

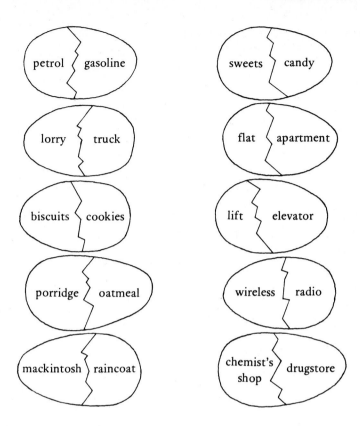

Variation: A similar activity may be done using other terms, such as CB (Citizen Band) terms:

Bear trap = speed trap   Front door = vehicle in front
Super slab = super highway   Green stamp = ticket
Smokey = policeman   Backdoor = vehicle behind
Ears = CB radio   Hammer = accelerator
Big 10–4 = acknowledged   Handle = CB nickname

See James L. Collier, *CB* (New York: Franklin Watts, 1977).

Language Changes

2.4 Two-Hundred-Year-Old Meanings (Intermediate)

Objective: To illustrate that language can change over a period of time.

Materials: Worksheet as suggested below.

Worksheet: Yesterday's and Today's Meaning

YESTERDAY	TODAY
Autopsy: seeing a thing one's self	*Autopsy*:
Catsup: a kind of Indian pickle, imitated by pickled mushroom.	*Catsup*:
Knave: a boy or servant	*Knave*:
Lunch: as much food as one's hand can hold	*Lunch*:
Minister: a servant	*Minister*:
Pioneer: a foot soldier	*Pioneer*:
Rum: a country parson	*Rum*:
Salvo: an exception or an excuse	*Salvo*:
Villain: a farmer	*Villain*:

Can you write pairs of sentences using each word to show its meaning over 200 years ago and its meaning today?

Directions: Directions for the activity are provided at the bottom of the chart. These words and definitions appeared in Samuel Johnson's *Dictionary of the English Language* (1755).

Variations:

1. After instruction, an activity can be designed to involve some of the specific ways in which words change in meaning. Some examples:

   Amelioration—formerly *enthusiastic* meant fanatic; currently, keen interest.

   Perjoration—formerly *villain* was a feudal serf; currently, a depraved scoundrel.

   Generalization—formerly *picture* meant only a painting; currently, it may be a print, photograph, a drawing.

   Specialization—formerly *meat* was any food; currently, mutton, pork, or beef.

2. Some other words that have changed meanings include:

1. whitewash	9. syrup	17. channel
2. marshall	10. parson	18. bank
3. do	11. silly	19. naughty
4. starve	12. lady	20. cunning
5. awful	13. paradise	21. fowl
6. undertaker	14. bishop	22. stool
7. salute	15. idiot	23. paper
8. ambition	16. fond	24. lumber

Students may plan an activity with the above set of words. Some sources students could consult are:

Adelson, Leone. *Dandelions Don't Bite: The Story of Words.* New York: Pantheon, 1972.

Davidson, Jessica. *Is That Mother in the Bottle? Where Language Comes From and Where It's Going.* New York: Franklin Watts, 1972.

Nurnburg, Maxwell. *Wonder in Words.* Englewood Cliffs, NJ: Prentice-Hall, 1968.

Language Variety

2.5   How Would You Say It? (Intermediate)

Objective: To help students recognize that language varies over geographic regions.

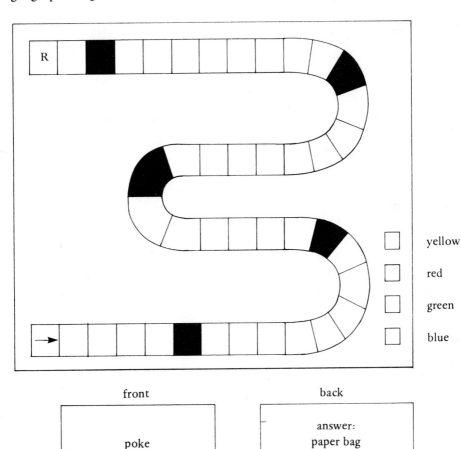

yellow

red

green

blue

front

back

poke

answer:
paper bag
(South)

Materials: A $2' \times 2'$ playing board as shown below. Four squares are colored to match card colors, a set of dice, markers for the children to use, and a stack of colored cards with word and answer as shown. Cards should include such regional terms, as these. (The first terms represent Appalachian regional usage.)

hose pipe—garden hose	snap beans—green beans
hot cakes—pancakes	coverlet—bedspread
pail—bucket	davenport—couch
corn pone—corn bread	bayou—brook
tote—carry	roasting ears—table corn
clabbered—sour	angleworm—earthworm
blinds—window shades	sinkers—doughnuts

Directions: After study of sets of regional words, this game is to be played with two to four players. The first player (to be decided by the highest roll of dice) rolls the dice and moves his or her marker to the number of squares indicated by the dice. If the player lands on a colored square, he or she picks a card of the same color from the stack on the board. The player reads the word on the card aloud, then gives the meaning of the term. If correct, the player remains on the square. If incorrect, the player goes back to the nearest unmarked square. The first player to reach the blue ribbon wins.

Variation: Use some of today's slang terms on the question cards. Some examples are:

rip off—steal	heavy—profound
far-out—great	right-on—to agree
goof-off—waste time	super—first-rate
cool—calm	funky—earthy
rap—talk	chalk up—to earn or score
hassle—argue	jiving—not telling the truth

LANGUAGE STRUCTURE

Suprasegmental: Intonation

2.6 Watch How You Say That! (Primary)

Objective: To help students realize that voice inflection affects meaning.

Materials: Sets of sentences with directions for reading as suggested.

Card 1

She is going   (indicates a fact)
                (expresses dislike of the idea)
                (emphasizes that action will be taken)
                (shows happiness about the information)

Card 2

Where is he going?
Where is he going?   (Not what or how)
Where *is* he going?   (Not was)
Where is *he* going?   (Not someone else)
Where is he *going*?   (Not eating, etc.)

Card 3

I did not say Bill hit the girl.

Can you change the stress on different words so you get six different meanings from this set of words?

Directions: Provide such sentences as the cards suggest and oral directions to the students. As one reads the cards aloud, others in the group suggest what is meant or not meant.

This activity could be played by teams. Pass out a slip of paper with a sentence with the key word underlined, as in Card 2. A child from one team reads the paper. A child from the other team must respond to what is *not* meant. The teacher or score-keeper counts the students in each team who answer correctly and records that number on the board for each team. Then a child from the other team follows the same procedure. After all have had a turn, the points are tallied.

Variations:

1. A single word, such as *Oh*, may be supplied to a student to read as if *hurt*; as if *surprised.*
2. Sentences may be furnished to be read in as many ways as possible to convey different meanings. Use such sentences as: "I said shut the door." "You are a real friend."

Homophones

2.7 Homophone Hunt (Primary)

Objective: To provide practice in recognition of homophones.

Materials: Chalkboard and chalk, picture dictionaries, and list of homophones.

Homophones

know	deer	hour	ate	flour
won	weak	knew	whole	rode
read	would	role	meat	it's
two	sent	see	write	sight

Directions: The students locate the matching word for the listed words, using their dictionaries if needed. The students may write or dictate a sentence containing each homophone. After completing the list provided, they may search for others not on the list.

Variation: The same "hunt" idea may be used for homographs (read, live), synonyms (sorrowful, unhappy), and antonyms (happy, sad).

Root Words and Prefixes

2.8 How Are the Words Related? (Intermediate)

Objective: To provide practice in determining word meanings by examining their structural parts—in this particular situation, common Latin and Greek roots and prefixes.

Materials: A work-sheet such as the following:

Worksheet: Questions of the Day

Use the information at the top of this page to help you answer the questions below.

tele—far; far off

telephone	phone	(sound, voice)
telegraph	graph	(to write)
television	vision	(sight; seeing)
telescope	scope	(instrument for observing)
telephoto	photo	(light)
telepathy	pathy	(feeling or perception)
telegram	gram	(thing written)
teletype	type	(printing)

1. What do these words have in common?
2. Try to define each word (using the dictionary if needed).
3. What do you think *tele-* of each word means?
4. How many other examples of words beginning with *tele-* can you give?

Directions: Procedures for the activity are provided at the bottom of the sheet.

Variation: Other sets of related words may be utilized, such as the following:

porter	script	automobile
export	manuscript	automatic
portable	scripture	autonomy
report	inscribe	autocrat
transport	prescribe	automation

Encourage use of an unabridged dictionary and perhaps provide a chart of some Latin and Greek roots and prefixes along with their common meanings as shown on illustrated sheet.

Figurative Language

2.9 What Curious Expressions (Intermediate)

Objective: To help students recognize figurative and idiomatic expressions.

Materials: Multiple copies of a story or poem containing many figures of speech. A sample passage is given below.

Walking in the Dark

Eric was shaking like a leaf on a tree. He had less than two hours to deliver the package before the axe fell. He was running around like a chicken with its head cut off. For one thing, he couldn't remember the address to save his life. For another, his car wouldn't go because the tires were flatter than pancakes.

Eric took off on foot like a shot out of a cannon. He went up and down each street on a wild goose chase. Each house he went to was the same old story. "Nobody is here by that name," they all told him, "why don't you make like a banana and split?"

Finally, he went to every house in the neighborhood with no success. He walked home slower than Christmas. When he got to his front porch, his mother was smiling like a Chesire cat.

"Oh, Eric, I'm so glad you brought the package home." his mother said, "because it has been a month of Sundays since I ordered it." Eric felt sillier than a square baseball bat. But he was happy anyway because the package had been delivered safely and everything was hunky dory.

Directions: The teacher reviews with the class the different types of figures of speech contained in the story or poem (for example, simile, metaphor, personification, hyperbole). Then the copies of the story are distributed. The students are instructed to locate as many figures of speech as they can, categorize each one, and give the literal meaning for each one. A time limit may be set, or the teacher may allow the students to work until everyone is finished. A student scores a point for each figure of speech identified, each correct category, and each correct literal meaning. Example: worked like a horse—simile—worked hard (3 points).

Variation: Students can read references that focus upon figurative and idiomatic expressions, as:

Ellentuck, Shan. *Did You See What I Said?* New York: Doubleday and Sons, 1967.

Funk, Charles E. *A Hog On Ice.* New York: Paperback Library, 1973.

Kohn, Bernice. *What a Funny Thing to Say.* New York: Dial Press, 1974.

———. *Spirit and the Letter.* New York: Viking Press, 1974.

LANGUAGE HISTORY

Hieroglyphics

2.10 Write a Rebus Story (Primary or Intermediate)

Objective: To introduce the concept of hieroglyphics.

Materials: A sample rebus story, as illustrated.

Key: The Star Mouse. One + ce (once) up + on (upon) a time,
a mouse went to the moon. The mouse used a balloon to go
to the moon. W + hen (when) he disc + overed (discovered)
t + hat (that) he was on the moon, he stuck a pin in the balloon.
The mouse fell back to the Earth. He was sad bee + cause
(because) the moon was not made of cheese.

Directions: Discuss the idea of a rebus story. Provide a sample as shown and ask the students to read it. Ask students to write a rebus story using such symbols.

Variation: This activity may involve writing in various forms—Indian, Chinese, Egyptian, or code writing. See such trade books as,

Amon, Aline. *Talking Hands: Indian Sign Language*. New York: Doubleday, 1968.

Katan, Norma. *Hieroglyphs: The Written Language of Ancient Egypt*. New York: Atheneum, 1981.

Peterson, John. *How to Write Codes and Secret Messages*. New York: Four Winds, 1970.

Weise, Kurt. *You Can Write Chinese*. New York: Viking, 1973.

Wolff, Diane, *Chinese Writing*. New York: Holt, Rinehart and Winston, 1975.

Historical Origins

2.11 How Did It Come to Mean? (Intermediate)

Objective: To provide practice in searching for original word meanings and relating them to current meaning.

Materials: An activity card, such as illustrated.

Some words are very old. Take the word *poet*, for example. The English borrowed it from the French language. But the French got the word from the Latin Language. And the people who spoke Latin got the word from the Greek language. In Greek, the word meant "maker." How can you think of a poet as a "maker"?

Trace the meaning of the following words back in time as far as you can and then write a paragraph about how the original meaning is related to the current meaning.

1. secure
2. train
3. ambition
4. character

Directions: Procedures for the activity are provided at the bottom of the activity card. Use reference materials such as Jo Ann

McCormack, *The Story of Our Language* (Columbus, OH: Charles E. Merrill, 1967) as well as dictionaries. Other excellent references on etymology include the following:

Epstein, Sam, and Beryl Epstein, *What's Behind the Word?* New York: Scholastic Book Services, 1964.

Funk, Charles E. *Heavens to Betsy!* New York: Warner Paperback Library, 1972.

Miller, Albert G. *Where Did That Word Come From?* Glendale, CA: Bowmer, 1974.

Severn, Bill. *People Words.* New York: Washburn, Inc., 1966.

Variations:

1. Students may be interested in finding the origins and meanings of their names. A valuable resource: Flora H. Loughead's *Dictionary of Given Names with Origins and Meanings* (Glendale, IL: The Arthur Clark Co., 1974); also see Elsdon C. Smith's *The Story of Our Names* (Detroit, MI: Gale, 1970); also see Ernest Klein's *A Comprehensive Etymological Dictionary of the English Language* (New York: Elsevier Publishing Co., 1971).

2. Students may be interested in an activity that involves learning about words that acquired their meanings in an unusual manner. Some such words are *nice, silly, knight, lady, barn, deer, corn, meat, handkerchief, pipe, chimney,* and *pencil.* A valuable resource: Albert G. Miller's *Where Did That Word Come From?* (Glendale, CA: Bowmar, 1976).

3. Students may be interested in an activity describing how places got their names (*chester, burg, ton, mont, ville, ford, haven, land, port, field, hill*), see Christine Fletcher, *100 Keys: Names Across the Land.* (Nashville, TN: Abingdon Press, 1973).

4. Students may wish to trace the derivation of names of days of the week and months of the year. See Isaac Asimov, *Words from the Myths* (Boston: Houghton Mifflin, 1961).

5. Students may use their dictionaries to determine the origins of "imported words": *pretzel, sauerkraut, hamburger, dessert, spaghetti, banana, frankfurter, dungaree, cafeteria, candy.*

6. Words from people's names could be explored: Colt, Levi, pasteurize, vulcanize, voltage, macintosh, and others.

Portmanteau Words

2.12 Blend the Words (Intermediate)

Objective: To provide practice with one way words are formed.

Materials: List of portmanteau words, index cards, felt-tip pen, and an example, as shown.

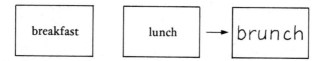

Directions: Instruct students to write words that are used to form portmanteau words on index cards:

bat + mash = bash
clap + crash = clash
flame + glare = flare
gleam + shimmer = glimmer
motor + hotel = motel
smoke + fog = smog

Explain the example. Mix up the cards. Instruct a student or pair of students or a small group to put together the cards to form portmanteau words. They write the words on an index card and place it beside the two original words.

Variation: Students can be encouraged to develop their own portmanteau words.

3 Grammar

Grammar is a description of the system by which language operates. Three major components of a grammar program in the language arts include parts of speech, sentence patterns, and sentence expansion and restructuring. The three sets of activities presented in this chapter are classified according to these components.

Traditional grammar arose over 400 years ago and described the English language in terms of Latin grammar. Traditional grammar in schools focused on categorizing the parts of speech in sentences and related activities. Traditionally, sentences have been categorized according to function (declarative, interrogative, imperative, and exclamatory) and structure (simple, compound, complex).

Structural grammar is the result of linguists' study of the way we speak. From this study, they devised different ways of defining form and function of words within sentences. For example, whereas the traditional grammarian defined a noun as the name of a person, place, or thing, the structural grammarian stated that a word is a noun because it can be made plural or possessive and may follow a determiner (*the, a, an,* etc). While structural grammar maintained the four major classes (noun, verb, adjective, and adverb), other categories for parts of speech were developed:

> *determiner* (or noun marker)—signals that a noun follows; includes articles, demonstrative pronouns, possessive pronouns, numbers, and so on: *My* brother caught *the* ball.
> *verb marker* (also called auxiliary)—signals that a verb follows
> *clause marker*—indicates a clause follows: because, if, how, etc.
> *phrase marker*—indicates a phrase follows: in, toward, etc.
> *intensifier* (or qualifier)—precedes adjectives and adverbs: very, just, etc.

The activities in the first section of this chapter illustrate concepts about parts of speech. The first one demonstrates that a word's part of speech cannot be divorced from its context; that is, an isolated word cannot be labeled as a particular part of speech. The second activity involves a basic belief of the structural grammarian—that position, form, and function will determine the part of speech. Other activities deal with selecting appropriate prepositions, differentiating adjectives and adverbs, recognizing contractions formed from a pronoun and a verb, and clarifying pronoun referents.

Perhaps one of the major contributions of structural grammar was the identification of basic sentence patterns in English. As a "refresher," here is one set of sentence patterns.

Pattern One

N-V (noun-verb): The airplane fell.
N-V-ad (noun-verb-adverb): Mary walked slowly.
N-V-adj (noun-verb-adjective): The man turned red.

Pattern Two

N-V-N (noun-verb-noun): The boy threw the ball.

Pattern Three

N-V-N-N (noun-verb-noun-noun): Dad called Tom a good helper.
N-V-N-adj (noun-verb-noun-adjective): Ruth painted the floor red.

Pattern Four

N-Lv-N (noun-linking verb-noun): My friend is an Englishman.
N-Lv-ad (noun-linking verb-adverb): Dot has been there.
N-Lv-adj (noun-linking verb-adjective): The apples were sour.
(Other linking verbs include *feel, seem, appear, look, become, remain, taste, smell, sound.*)

The second part of this chapter provides several activities dealing with the concept of sentence pattern. Activities involve, first, constructing sentences in preset patterns and then developing the recognition of particular patterns.

The third part of this chapter focuses upon sentence expansion and restructuring. This feature of grammar study is a part of *transformational-generative grammar.* Transformational grammar speaks of two basic types of sentences: kernel and transformed.

Kernel sentences are simple, declarative, active sentences. All other sentences are transformed from the kernel sentences.

Kernel: The boy bought an apple.
Transformed passive: An apple was bought by the boy.
Transformed negative: The boy did not buy an apple.
Transformed question: Did the boy buy an apple?
Transformed negative-passive-question: Was not an apple bought by the boy?
Transformed by expansion: The boy in the green sweater bought a large red apple.

Furthermore, coordination of kernel sentences is possible:

The boy bought an apple.
His father bought an apple.
The boy and his father bought apples.

The third set of activities deals with sentence order and expansion, joining related sentences, writing and placing adverbial modifiers, and transforming sentences.

All the activities in this chapter may be approached as concept explorations rather than as skills to be mastered.

For readers who wish more information about the basic types of grammar, the following references can be consulted.

Bolinger, Dwight L. *Aspects of Language*, 2d. ed. New York: Harcourt, Brace, and World, 1975.

Herndon, Jeanne H. *A Survey of Modern Grammars*, 2d. ed. New York: Holt, Rinehart and Winston, 1976.

Hook, J.N., and Michael G. Crowell. *Modern English Grammar for Teachers*. New York: Ronald, 1970.

Langacker, Ronald W. *Language and Its Structure: Some Fundamental Linguistic Concepts*, 2d. ed. New York: Harcourt, Brace, Jovanovich, 1973.

Malmstrom, Jean. *Grammar Basics*, 2d. ed. Rochelle Park, NJ: Hayden Book Company, 1977.

_____. *Understanding Language: A Primer for the Language Arts Teacher*. New York: St. Martin's, 1977.

Stageberg, Norman C. *An Introductory English Grammar*, New York: Holt, Rinehart and Winston, 1971.

Thomas, Owen P. *Transformational Grammar and the Teacher of English*. New York: Holt, Rinehart and Winston, 1965.

Weaver, Constance. *Grammar for Teachers*. Urbana, IL: NCTE, 1979.

PARTS OF SPEECH

3.1 Noun or Verb? (Primary or Intermediate)

Objective: To help students distinguish between a word used as a noun or as a verb.

Materials: A game board as illustrated, bottle caps for markers, dice, and a list of words to put on index cards.

drive paint walk
sleep farm   camp
step   park   talk

Directions: This game can be played with two or three players. The first player rolls the die and moves the number of spaces shown on the die. He or she picks a card from the stack. If the space is marked *n*, the player must use the word as a noun in a sentence. If the space is marked *v* the player must use the word as a verb. For example, *talk* as a noun: Did you have a *talk* with her? and as a verb: Did you *talk* with her?

3.2 Nonsense Nouns and Verbs (Intermediate)

Objective: To develop students' ability to identify words used as nouns or used as verbs based on position, form, and function.

Materials: Sentences such as the following:

A garlun pommels its triman.
Several garluns pommelled their trimans.
Two beelors gave the ruting some tavery.
Every dresh is a misdottle.
A dresh can foerlize those bandorps.

Directions: Provide a selection to each student. Ask them to draw one line under each noun and two lines under each verb. Discuss the reasons for their responses.

Variation: Activities may be developed around other determinants of the parts of speech commonly presented at the elementary school level:

Nouns	*Verbs*
Singular/plural (regular/irregular)	Helping
Common/proper	Linking
Possessive (singular/plural)	Agreement with subject
Direct object or predicate noun	Tense (regular/irregular)

For example, an activity which involves the use of irregular verbs can ask a series of questions:

Where did you begin? (requesting a *began* or *begun* answer)
What did you wear?
What did you draw?
What did you catch?
What did you drink?
What did you see?

3.3 Missing Prepositions (Intermediate)

Objective: To provide practice in using prepositions.

Materials: A selection such as suggested here.

On the Road

(8) the bad weather, Phillip kept going *(21)* his goal. *(4)* it started raining, he made the decision to continue. *(10)* the trip, he felt unsure because the car made noises *(2)* a few miles.

(9) the road, Phillip saw a truck *(13)* trouble *(23)* flares *(3)* the back wheels. He pulled *(18)* the road and stopped *(5)* the truck.

The truck driver came *(12)* the side *(17)* the road and stood *(6)* Phillip's car. He said, "Thanks *(11)* stopping but every thing is OK *(14)* my truck."

Phillip got back *(19)* the road and drove *(22)* he made it *(1)* the state line. He finally stopped *(7)* a river *(16)* the road. He slept *(20)* the night and *(15)* the next day.

1. across	8. despite	16. near
2. after	9. down	17. of
3. around	10. during	18. off
4. before	11. for	19. on
5. behind	12. from	20. throughout
6. beside	13. in	21. toward
7. by	14. inside	22. until
	15. into	23. with

Directions: Distribute copies of the material. Ask the students to read the passage and fill in each blank with the number of the preposition from the listing of prepositions at the bottom of the page. (The appropriate numbers are supplied for the sample selection.) When they have finished, discuss with them the appropriateness of the prepositions they have chosen. Ask them what helped them decide which preposition to use. Accept all meaningful responses.

Variation: A similar activity could be developed for other parts of speech.

3.4 Adjective or Adverb? (Intermediate)

Objective: To help students differentiate adjectives and adverbs.

Materials: Poster of ideas about adjectives and adverbs:

Adjectives

1. Describe noun: the *tall* boy
2. Comparison: young, younger, youngest; beautiful, more beautiful, most beautiful
3. Proper noun: the *Japanese* car
4. Predicate adjective: The boy is *strong*.

Adverbs

1. Describe verb, adjective, or another adverb: worked *quickly*
2. Comparison: fast, faster, fastest; carefully, more carefully, most carefully
3. Tells how, when, where

---

and a set of sentences:

1. The water is hot.
2. Joe walked carefully.
3. The noisy children went away.
4. The boy is short.
5. The girl is here.
6. The strongest student is Betty.
7. Tom plays hard.
8. The American flag was waving in the air.
9. Jill arrived sooner than Janet.
10. The cake is sweet.

Directions: After reviewing the poster of ideas, ask the students to underline each adjective in the set of sentences and circle each adverb. When they finish, let them compare answers, citing reasons for their markings.

Variation: Individual items from the poster may be practiced through various activities. For example, for the idea of *comparison* let three students stand before the class. Two will mark on the chalkboard as high as they can reach. The third student will ask the class: "Who marked the higher? Who made the longer mark?" Let the same two students step as far as they can in one step, followed by appropriate questions. Or let them stand back to back, with the questions, "Who is the taller? Who is the shorter?" Three students could be actors when providing practice for the *superlative* degree.

3.5 Pronouns and Verbs Contracted (Primary or Intermediate)

Objective: To provide practice with contractions formed from a pronoun and a verb.

Materials: Duplicating master and a typewriter or pen.

Match!

Directions: Find the short form that matches each of the long forms. Place the letter of the short form beside the number of the long form.

Long Form	Short Form
_____ 1. you have	a. we've
_____ 2. I am	b. we're
_____ 3. She is	c. she's
_____ 4. we are	d. I've
_____ 5. you will	e. you'll
_____ 6. I have	f. I'm
_____ 7. let us	g. you've
_____ 8. he had	h. they've
_____ 9. they have	i. you're
_____ 10. we have	j. he'd
_____ 11. you are	k. let's

Directions: Prepare a duplicating master as illustrated. Distribute copies of the sheet to the students. Direct them to write the letter of the short form that matches the long form. Discuss the exercise after the students have completed it.

Variation: Activities may be developed around pronoun concepts commonly presented at the elementary school level: subjects, direct objects, objects of preposition, possessives. For example, here is an idea for pronouns as subjects. Two forms of a sentence are written on a slip and put in a bag: "He and I are going." and "Me and him are going." The question on the slip asks, "Which is correct?" The class is divided into two teams. Each player on the team is given a chance to draw a slip from the bag and give an answer. Each correct answer counts one point, and the team with more points is declared winner.

3.6 To What Does It Refer? (Primary)

Objective: To develop awareness of pronoun referents.

Materials: Duplicating paper, typewriter or felt-tip pen, and sets of sentences.

Read each sentence. Then draw an arrow, as shown in the example, from each underlined pronoun to the word it refers to.

Sam and *his* friend told Mary that *they* would take *her* for a ride in the car.

1. Bill pointed to the table and asked Jim to help *him* move it.
2. Bill said *he* would swim and Mary said *she* would dive.
3. "*We* are glad *you* came to visit *us*, Jim," the children told *him*.
4. The teacher told the children that *they* had made *her* very proud.
5. Missy asked Mr. Hill to tell *her* what color *he* was going to paint *his* boat.

Directions: The directions are provided at the top of the worksheet. After the students have completed the exercises, they should discuss their responses.

SENTENCE PATTERNS

3.7 Connect Subject and Predicate (Primary)

Objective: To develop familiarity with basic sentence patterns.

Materials: Worksheets, as illustrated.

A

NP	VP
Snow	is green.
Jean	was bit by the dog.
The grass	is sour.
He	is white.
Lemon	is tall.

B

NP	VP
The planes	bury bones.
The horses	is running.
She	are landing.
The girls	have saddles.
The dogs	are swimming.

C

NP		VP
She	ran	over the net.
The car	bounced	off the road.
The ball	looks	from the shelf.
A book	were	very nice.
We	fell	at the game.

Directions: Ask the students to use the set of words in Box A to see how many sentences they can make. The same directions would be given for boxes B and C. Accept all reasonable responses.

Variation: Give each student two small cards. Put *S* on one to represent sentence and *X* on the other to represent not a sentence. As the teacher reads a sentence or a fragment, each student holds up the appropriate card.

3.8 Create a Sentence (Intermediate)

Objective: To develop familiarity with the structural components of sentences.

Materials: Four word lists, as suggested below:

Nouns	Verbs	Adjectives	Adverbs
car	ran	wild	fast
crow	jumped	tiny	painfully
cat	played	crazy	beautifully
bicycle	spoke	long	happily
dog	limped	naughty	softly
kite	danced	huge	noisily
fly	glides	red	slowly
girl	laughed	silly	loudly
clown	creaked	beautiful	away
plane	raced	careless	easily

Directions: Place the lists on the bulletin board. Ask students to create as many sensible sentences as possible, using one word from each list and adding needed words. At other times they may be requested to create humorous sentences. At other times, students may suggest adjectives, nouns, adverbs, and verbs to be used in the lists.

3.9 Pattern Squares (Intermediate)

Objective: To increase familiarity with the structural patterns of sentences, in this case four basic patterns of the declarative sentences.

Materials: Poster board marked off in nine squares (tic-tac-toe) as illustrated, five or six x's and o's made from construction paper; and a box containing papers with declarative sentences of four basic types (answers on back)

1	2	3
4	5	6
7	8	9

1. N-V   / The sun shines.
2. N-V-N   / Mother baked cookies.
3. N-V-N-N / Bill gave Susie a ring.
4. N-V-N′   / Jimmy is the class president.

Directions: This game is played as the television program "Hollywood Squares." Two players try to get three squares in a row either diagonally, horizontally, or vertically. Nine students are the "actors" for the squares. The players each choose a square and the person designated for that square. The narrator or teacher draws one sentence from the box and the "star" tells which basic pattern the sentence is. The player then decides whether the sentence is correct or if it is a bluff. If the player is correct, he or she gets an x or an o in the box chosen. If the answer is incorrect, the opponent gets the square unless it would give three in a row. The game continues until one player wins the designated number of games; then another player takes the loser's place. This game should also be developed for other structured patterns.

3.10 What Kind of Sentence? (Primary)

Objective: To facilitate recognition of sentence functions.

Materials: Set of cards for each player, as:

Tells something .	Asks a question ?	Shows strong feeling or surprise !

Sets of different kinds of sentences, as

Will you please sit down?
What a wonderful surprise!
Jean has blue eyes.

Directions: Divide the players into two teams. Pass out one set of cards for each player. The teacher reads a set of sentences one at a time. Then the students in Team A hold up the card for the type of sentence read. The teacher counts the number of students in Team A who answered correctly and records that number. Then this procedure is used with Team B. After a number of rounds, the points are tallied and the winning team is announced.

Variation: Other activities may be developed around other sentence concepts commonly presented at the elementary school level: subject and predicate; subject and verb agreement; simple and complete subjects; simple and complete predicates; compound subjects; compound predicates; compound sentences.

SENTENCE EXPANSION AND RESTRUCTURING

Sentence Expansion

3.11 Expand the Sentence (Intermediate)

Objective: To provide experience in expanding sentences.

Materials: Cut apart a sentence by putting one word on each card. Make two copies of each word on 8″ × 11″ cards. Some blank cards.

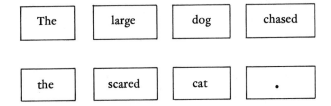

Directions: This game is to be played with two teams. The team leader selects the same number of players to participate as there are words in the sentence, plus one. (In sentence above, eight players are needed.) At the signal, selected players from each team take a card and organize themselves facing the other students in an order that makes a sentence. The group that forms a sentence first scores three points. Other team members can score one point by writing a word on a blank card and adding it to the sentence already formed. Each team is given three chances to do this. After three sentences the team with the most points wins.

Variation: Students holding cards may tell what part of speech their word represents.

3.12 Combine the Sentences (Primary or Intermediate)

Objective: To provide practice with sentence combining; that is, joining two related sentences into one.

Materials: Set of sentence pairs.

1. The girl sang.
   The girl was pretty.
   The pretty girl sang.
2. The shirt has long sleeves.
   The shirt was blue.
3. The girl ate a hamburger.
   The girl went to a movie.
4. The cat purred.
   The cat was resting on the blanket.
5. Jim has a dog.
   The dog is frisky.
6. David is my cousin.
   He moved to Minnesota.

Directions: Present a sample pair of sentences on the overhead projector and show the combined sentence. Ask, "What was done?" Orally give a series of short sentences and call for individual responses. When it is clear to students, a worksheet composed of sets of sentences may be distributed with instructions to combine the sentences. (The sample sentences cited in "Materials" involve compounding the subject, predicate, using relative clause, possessives, and appositive.) Oral discussion may follow.

Variation:

1. Sentence combining involving coordinators, subordinators, and connectors may be utilized for more advanced students.
2. Sentence combining involving the students' own compositions would be especially effective at the early and middle intermediate grades.

Sentence Restructuring

3.13 When, Where, and How? (Intermediate)

Objective: To provide experience in using adverbial modifiers and moving them about within a sentence for variety.

Materials: Long strip of paper about 3″ × 24″, narrow pieces of paper (different colors) 1″ × 6″, pencils, paper clips.

Cars go	

Where?	When?	How?

Cars go	slowly	on the interstate	at the rush hour

Directions: Provide the beginning noun and verb, such as "Cars go." On the first 1″ × 6″ paper slip, the student writes a phrase telling *where* something happened. On the second slip, the student writes a phrase telling *when* something happened. On the third

1" × 6" slip, the student writes a word about *how* it was done. The student then clips on the three cards where they make the best sense. Students read their sentences aloud and practice moving the phrases.

3.14 Change the Sentence! (Intermediate)

Objective: To introduce and to begin to explore the concept of transformational grammar.

Materials: Duplication master, typewriter or pen, and a series of sentences, as illustrated.

Figure It Out!

Study the transformed sentences. Then transform each of the sentences at the bottom of the page as directed.

1. He is a good player.   He is not a good player.
2. She drove the car.   She did not drive the car.
3. They are eating dinner at 5:00.   Are they eating dinner at 5:00?
4. They went to church.   Did they go to church?
5. You answer the phone.   Answer the phone.
6. She works hard.   Work hard.
7. A kitten is in her room.   There is a kitten in her room.
8. Bradly bought the bike.   The bike was bought by Bradly.
9. Betty has a cat.   My dog chased Betty's cat.
   My dog chased the cat.

---

1. The ball is blue.   (NEGATIVE)
2. She is tall.   (NEGATIVE)
3. They are going to the party.   (QUESTION)
4. Tom is pitching.   (QUESTION)
5. You cook the steaks.   (REQUEST)
6. You drive the car.   (REQUEST)
7. A racket is in the closet.   (THERE)
8. A car hit the dog.   (PASSIVE)
9. Bill has a dog.
   My book fell on the dog.   (POSSESSIVE)

Directions: Procedures for the activity are suggested at the top of the worksheet. Discuss answers and the transformation of each sentence.

4 Pre- or Early School Language Arts

Young children have acquired competence in language by the time they enter the first grade; language grows at its most rapid rate in the early years. This is generally regarded as a crucial time for the child's language development to be stimulated and enriched.

By the time children reach school age they will have passed through several developmental stages and tried out several learning styles. In the earliest stage, infants learn by waving their arms and legs in the air, the first sign of the kinesthetic or motor modality of learning. Very soon thereafter the child begins to learn by touching everything nearby, which is the start of the tactile modality of learning. By the time the child has reached six months of age, the senses of hearing and seeing become increasingly refined, thereby enabling the child to use the auditory and visual modalities of learning. These modalities are never completely phased out, though there is a later shift in emphasis to the visual and the auditory modalities as the child learns to read and to listen attentively.

This chapter includes activities organized around each of the four learning modalities: motor, tactile, auditory, and visual. Some activities use these modalities to stimulate the development of language abilities and skills. For example, through the motor activities presented in the first section of the chapter, children are stimulated in such language areas as interpreting actions, "acting out" in such a way that others may interpet the action or situation, remembering a sequence, "reading" emotions, associating words and emotions, demonstrating word meanings, and interpreting motive words. Such bodily motions are expressive, just as language is expressive; both provide opportunity for communication. In brief, such motor activity, often accompanied by verbal expressions, increases recall, discriminative listening, and forms of communication. In a similar manner, language development may be enhanced by tactile sensory input where words are attached to shapes, sizes, weights, and textures.

The largest section in this chapter is devoted to activities related to the auditory and visual modalities. The young student needs to develop a variety of auditory and visual skills such as general listening comprehension, following directions, active attentive listening, auditory discrimination, "reading" pictures, and "picturing" in the mind.

Additional attention is given in this chapter to a few suggestions for activities where language development may be enhanced by the senses of smell and taste. These modalities have been generally ignored in research. However, research as well as personal experience does indicate that the senses of taste and smell are frequent stimulators of language; and they are certainly a very important part of the experiences of everyday living, especially for the young child.

The next section of this chapter deals with the alphabet. During the early years the preschool child first encounters this abstract concept and is often fascinated by it—what the forms are, what each of them stands for, what they do, why they exist, and, later, why there are lots of them put together in bunches (words) that they see on signs, in stores, in books, and everywhere they go. The student's knowledge of the alphabet is a reliable predictor of later reading achievement.[1] Although this does not mean that teaching preschool students the alphabet will guarantee their later success in learning to read, it does indicate that the alphabet is an important concept. Knowledge of the alphabet may be helpful to the beginning reader because (1) letters of the alphabet are often associated with the sounds which are encountered in listening and reading, and (2) the alphabet begins to establish a mental concept of written language, which will develop dramatically as students encounter print in functional situations. The alphabet is also important in analyzing and teaching essential prereading phonics skills.

The concluding section of this chapter presents an overview of the Language Experience Approach and provides references for specific activities associated with this idea. In many ways, though, the modality activities in this chapter are a part of the Language Experience Approach.

There are many activities for increasing awareness of all we learn through our senses throughout life. Ideas from this chapter may be modified to be appropriate for older students.

---

[1]Donald D. Durrell, "Letter Name Values in Reading and Spelling," *Reading Research Quarterly* 16, no. 1 (1980): 159-163.

MOTOR MODALITY

4.1 What Am I Doing?

Objective: To stimulate oral language development by physical action.

Materials: List of everyday situations to be acted out: making a bed, tying shoes, cooking a pancake, brushing teeth, combing hair; and more involved activities such as nailing two boards together and sawing the ends off; painting a picture, holding it in front of yourself, turning it upside down, placing it back on the easel, backing away from it to look again. Other simple activities could include knitting, sneezing, crying, hiding from someone, telling a secret to a friend, and eating lunch.

Directions: Act out an everyday activity after instructing the students to guess what is being acted out. Then whisper an activity to a student who then acts out the activity while the others guess what is being done. (If preferred, the class can act out the situation.)

4.2 Happy, Sad, Silly, and Glad!

Objective: To increase vocabulary of emotion words and words related to emotions.

Materials: List of emotional words, such as

happy	joyful	disgusted	shy
sad	mischievous	eager	hoping
angry	confused	embarrassed	hurt
tired	silly	friendly	glad

Directions: Act out a chosen emotion. The students are to try to guess the feeling. Then the students get an opportunity to act out an emotion word.

Whisper the word to the first player. The student then acts out the chosen emotion word until one of the others guesses it. If no one guesses after a reasonable amount of time, the player selects another to do the next word. If a student who has not had a turn guesses the word, then that student is next to act out an emotion word; if the student has already had a turn, then the privilege earned is to select the next player who will act out an emotion word.

4.3 How Am I Moving?

Objective: To present vocabulary of action verbs using physical involvement with the words.

Materials: List of action words:

walk	gallop	slide	jump
skip	crawl	twist	stomp
run	hop	turn	droop

Directions: Explain that students are going to act out different ways to move. Whisper one word to a student, such as "walk." Then walk a few steps with student and stop. Any student who has an idea of what the word is whispers to teacher. If the answer is correct, that student also gets to "walk" when teacher and student demonstrate again. After four or five rounds (or fewer if all the students guess the word correctly) the word is told aloud, in unison, to the entire group. Then everyone gets to demonstrate the word together before going on to a new action word.

4.4 Move with Perky

Objective: To stimulate language development through kinesthetic participation.

Materials: Stories that include movements that can be acted out as the story is being read.

Perky Learns a Lesson

Perky was a bunny rabbit. He loved to hop forwards . . . he loved to hop backwards . . . he loved to hop sideways. Sometimes he would even turn circles while he hopped. Perky's very favorite trick was to lie down and pretend he was asleep. Then when anyone came near he would hop up right in front of them and startle them. Then Perky would laugh because he thought he was the greatest animal in the world!

One day his mother asked, "Perky, I know you can hop very well. But can you move like the other animals do?" Well, Perky didn't know if he could or not but he was willing to try.

So, he went for a walk. He saw a duck waddling and he tried to waddle. But he couldn't waddle. Then he saw a dog running and he tried to run. But he couldn't run like the dog. He also saw a squirrel climb up a tree. When he tried to climb the tree, he just fell down.

Perky saw a bird fly but when he tried to fly, it only made his ears tired. He saw a horse gallop but he fell on his nose when he tried to gallop. And last, he saw a fish swimming. When he tried to swim, though, he just splashed and got soaked through and through.

Perky was very sad. He went back to his mother and said, "Mother, I'm not a very good bunny. I can't waddle like the duck. I can't run like the dog. I can't climb a tree like the squirrel. I can't gallop like the horse. I can't swim like the fish. I guess I'm not a very good bunny. All I can do is hop." Perky looked like he was about to cry.

Then his mother spoke up and said, "Perky, I'm glad you learned your lesson. You see, no one can do everything well. But everyone is important because each one can do something no one else can. So, remember that all the other animals are important, too. And *you* are important because you can hop!"

This made Perky so happy that he hopped all over the place! He hopped forwards. He hopped backwards. He hopped sideways. He even hopped in circles!

Now Perky is a very happy Bunny!

Directions: Read the story aloud. The students act out or move to the story details as it is read to them.

TACTILE MODALITY

4.5 Feel and Describe

Objective: To stimulate the students' descriptive vocabulary development.

Materials: Such objects as:

kitten	sponge
ice cube	cottonball
pine cone	velvet or velour
cocklebur	burlap bag

feather   snakeskin
hair   football
fork   clay

Directions: An object is passed to one student. That student rubs the object and with each stroke says a word which describes the object. When that student can no longer think of any words, the object is passed on to another who rubs and describes the object. (The teacher can choose whether it is best to allow words to be repeated.)

4.6 Touch and Tell the Blind Puppet

Objective: To stimulate oral language by tactile senses.

Materials: A hand puppet or finger puppet (or other puppet which can easily be manipulated) and various objects for the students to touch.

Directions: The student receives or makes a puppet and is told that the puppet is blind. The student is then instructed to help the puppet know what some everyday items are like. This is accomplished by the student telling how the item feels. The student may wear the puppet on one hand and feel with the other. Dialogue between the student and puppet is encouraged.

Variation: Have the student wear the puppet on one hand and then blindfold the student. An unfamiliar object is presented to the student and the *puppet* then describes what the object feels like.

AUDITORY MODALITY

4.7 Do What I Say

Objective: To develop listening skills and the ability to remember and follow directions in sequence.

Materials: List of "Do What I Say" tasks:

tie shoes	sing a note	turn around
walk to the door	clap hands	bend over
hop on one foot	wave arms	point a finger

Directions: The teacher explains that students are to play a "follow-the-teacher's direction" game. The teacher then states a small task. After several times of using one directional task, the teacher states two tasks to be carried out in order, before the next set of directions. The number of tasks in each set of directions is increased until the students reach their limit. (Use specific sequence cues—first, second, third—for multistep tasks.)

4.8 Hear and Tell

Objective: To stimulate imaginative thinking and oral language.

Materials: Various recordings of music and sound effects.

Directions: The teacher plays a recording. Afterwards, one of the following questions is asked: What happened? Would you tell a story about what you heard? Who is in this? Where is this taking place?

4.9 Sing a Story

Objective: To stimulate listening and speaking skills by using singing.

Materials: Various short stories, fairy tales, or nursery rhymes.

Directions: Read or recite a familiar story to the students. The next step is to have each student "sing" the story. This will be an impromptu sing-song type of song. (Teacher may need to demonstrate.)

Variations:
1. All of the children can sing the story together to get the children started.
2. This activity can be done in reverse, also: a familiar song is sung and then the student retells the story without singing it.

4.10 Use Your Fingers—and Thumb

Objective: To provide listening comprehension experience.

Materials: The following story (or similar kinds of stories).

Johnny and Sue Thumb

Johnny Thumb felt as if he had no friends. He was so sad he was bent over. Every day he looked over at all the other children and wondered why he couldn't be a part of the games they played. Sally was wiggling and dancing, and Chris was riding on an up-and-down swing. Joe and Jake looked as if they were wrestling with each other. And Sue Thumb was having the grandest time of all, going back and forth and round and behind, seeing what was going on. Then he saw all of them playing at once. What a happy time they must be having! But what a shame that he couldn't play with them.

Then from behind he heard a voice, "Johnny Thumb, would you like to play with us? We are very near you and we would love to have you join us!" Johnny Thumb turned around and there he saw Jane and Karen wrestling together! He saw Scott riding an up-and-down swing. And Ronnie was also dancing to the new song he had just learned. They were all playing and having such a grand time together! When Johnny Thumb joined them, he knew he was the happiest thumb in the world! Now Johnny never even thinks about being sad any more because he has his own special friends with him! And they *all* played happily with their friends.

Directions: The story above is read aloud. As each new character is introduced, hold up the correct finger and wiggle it appropriately. When the story is reread, the students move the appropriate finger.

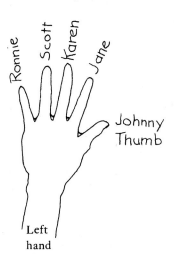

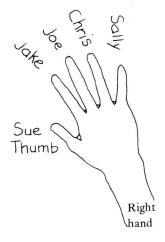

4.11 Move Your Body

Objective: To provide experience in listening and following directions.

Materials: Index cards and movement poems.

Movement
Touch your toes.
Straighten up.
Touch your toes again.
Place your hands upon your head.
Break into a grin.
Swing your arms from side to side.
Stand up straight and tall, with pride.

Directions: Make a collection of "movement poems" such as the one above. The students use their bodies to illustrate the meanings of words as the teacher reads the poem.

4.12 Listen—and Make the Sound

Objective: To provide listening experiences which involve students as active participants.

Materials: A story similar to the example.

A Day's Beginning

One night, when all was quiet in the house except for the cat purring and the fire crackling, something strange happened. The grandfather clock down the hallway began chiming.

Just as the clock struck six everything started happening! It sounded like the wind started blowing, and rain began pouring down! Then a soldier came out from hiding and started blowing his bugle! And then two dancers came out of the door and began dancing, while some singers began singing a song!

Finally, the clock finished striking six. Upstairs a lady rolled in bed and looked at her clock. Sure enough, it was six o'clock. She said to her husband, "The cuckoo in the grandfather clock says that it's time to get up."

And so, they got up. You see, all of the dancers, the singers, and the soldier were part of the grandfather cuckoo clock. And the wind and the rain were just part of the teapot.

Then the cat got up and walked over to listen to the fire. He purred loudly for his breakfast. Yes, it certainly was time for the brand new day to begin!

Directions: Explain that students are to make the sound of what they hear each time they hear it. The students may move as the dancers and speak the dialogue between the woman and her husband.

Variation: Here are a few trade books for use as sound stories:
Baylor, Byrd. *Plink, Plink, Plink.* Boston: Houghton Mifflin. 1971.
Brown, Margaret Wise. *Noisy Book.* New York: Harper and Row, 1939.
_____. *Indoor Noisy Book.* New York: Harper and Row, 1941.
_____. *Country Noisy Book.* New York: Harper and Row, 1940.
_____. *The Seashore Noisy Book.* New York: Harper and Row, 1940.
_____. *The Quiet Noisy Book.* New York: Harper and Row, 1950.
_____. *The Winter Noisy Book.* New York: Harper and Row, 1967.
Elkin, Benjamin. *The Loudest Noise in the World.* New York: Viking, 1954.
Gaeddert, Lou Ann. *Noisy Nancy Norris.* New York: Doubleday, 1971. (Also see *Noisy Nancy and Nick,* 1971)
Hanson, Joan. *Sound Words: Words that Imitate the Sounds Around.* Minneapolis: Lerner, 1976.
Johnson, LaVerne. *Night Noises.* New York: Parents Magazine Press, 1968.
Johnston, Tony. *High Noises and Other Mole and Troll Series.* New York: G.P. Putnam's Sons, 1977.
Kuskin, Karla. *All Sizes of Noises.* New York: Harper and Row, 1962.
McGovern, Ann. *Too Much Noise.* Boston: Houghton Mifflin, 1967.
O'Neill, Mary. *What Is That Sound?* New York: Atheneum, 1966.
Perkins, Al. *The Ear Book.* New York: Random House, 1968.
Seuss, Dr. *Mr. Brown Can Moo, Can You?* New York: Random House, 1977.
Slepian, Jan, and Ann Seidler. *The Silly Listening Book.* Chicago: Follett, 1967.

Spier, Peter. *Crash! Bang! Boom!* New York: Doubleday, 1972.
Steiner, Charlotte. *Listen to My Seashell.* New York: Knopf, 1959.
Wells, Rosemary. *Noisy Nora.* New York: Dial, 1973.

4.13 Solve the Riddle

Objective: To provide auditory comprehension experiences.

Materials: Index cards with riddles printed on them.

> I am an animal. I use only two legs to walk on, like you. If I want to go somewhere fast, though, I don't walk—I jump. Also, if I have a baby, I carry it around with me all the time. What am I?

> I am a grown-up, and my job is very interesting. All day long I talk or play records! You can never see me, but you can hear me anytime you want. I can't hear you, though, unless you call me up on the phone. In fact, with a little button, you can decide how loud you want me to talk, and whether or not you want to hear me at all. Who am I?

> I'm sitting at a table now. In my hand I have a small bottle that is full. I am holding it over my plate of food. I am turning the bottle partly upside-down and shaking it over my food. What am I doing?

> The sun feels so good! Also, it feels good to be walking on sand, except when I step on a sharp shell. The best thing, though, is the water! Where am I?

What I see is red, and it has four wheels and a ladder and a siren. It is making a lot of fuss and is rushing down the road! What do I see?

Directions: Read the riddles and ask the students to guess the answer. Discussion of the clues may be appropriate.

Variation: Supply one clue (one sentence) and let the students guess after each clue.

4.14 Fill in the Story

Objective: To encourage attentive critical listening.

Materials: A story such as the following.

Tom and His Wish

Once there was a little boy with red hair. His name was Tom. Tom lived out on a farm and helped his old grandmother and grandfather raise _____. He was a very happy little boy except for one thing: he wished he had a mother and father like all the other boys and girls.

One day, the king and queen of the country were passing through. They saw the little _____ and his _____ and _____ working out in the _____. So they stopped to say "Hi."

The king called out, "Hello, Mr. Farmer! Hello, Mrs. Farmer!"

The queen called out, "Good afternoon, Mrs. Farmer! Good afternoon, Mr. Farmer!"

The little _____ was very excited. His grandmother and grandfather called back to the _____ and _____. "Hello, Your Highness! Hello, Your Majesty!"

Then the king saw the little boy, who was also working on the _____. "My, what a fine boy you have here!" said the _____.

The grandfather said, "Thank you. We are proud of him."

The queen asked, "What is your name, little boy?"

He replied, "My name is _____."

"What a nice _____," replied the _____.

Then the king and queen started whispering together about something. In a moment the king looked up and said to the grandmother and _____ and to _____, "We like you very much. And we have decided to grant Tom a wish."

The queen looked at Tom and asked, "Tom, if you had one _____, what would you want?"

Tom thought a moment and said, "I wish that I could have a mother and father like everyone else."

The king and _____ looked puzzled at each other. How could they grant Tom's wish? Then they thought of an idea and began whispering to one another.

Then the king spoke, "Tom, you already have a _____ and _____. They treat you like you were their own real son, so, you see, you really have your parents."

Tom looked very sad when he heard this. But then the queen spoke up. "Tom," she said, "we like you. And we don't have any _____. So, we thought you could come live with us and be our little _____ during the winter months. You could even go to school in the Royal Palace, and learn many wonderful things."

The king added, "Yes, and then during the summer you could come back to be with your _____ and _____ and help them raise _____ on the _____." The king continued, "Would you like to be our little _____, Tom?"

Tom was so happy, he could not even talk. So he rushed over and hugged them.

Then, as the king and _____ had to leave, the king said, "Tom, we want you to work very hard on the _____ because your _____ and _____ have been very good to you. Then in the fall we will come back and take you to school in the Royal Palace."

Tom replied, "Yes, sir. I will work very hard. And I will love my _____ and _____."

The king and _____ turned to go. "Good-bye!" said the king and queen. "See you in the fall!"

"Good-bye!" said the grandmother and _____.

"Good-bye!" said Tom. And he waved good-bye to the _____ and _____ until they were out of sight.

Directions: Read the story aloud. When an omitted word is reached, indicate that the students are to fill in the word. The students then supply the word, discuss briefly their reasons for their choices, and the story continues.

4.15 Complete the Rhyme

Objective: To provide practice with auditory discrimination skills involving rhyming.

Materials: Index cards with rhyming couplets printed on them.

> The robin flew up into the sky
> I could not see it, it went so _____.

> The beautiful roses were so red
> That were planted in my flower _____.

> If you're running a race and don't want to be last,
> You can't run slow, you've got to run _____.

> I had a duck and put it in a sack,
> But it was unhappy and it cried _____, _____!

Directions: Read the rhyming couplets aloud, omitting the final words of each second line. The students orally supply the missing words based on contextual clues and rhyming patterns.

Variation: Students can also supply words which fit the context but do not rhyme. Then the rhyming words can be identified as fitting the sentence better.

VISUAL MODALITY

4.16 Tell the Story with Pictures

Objective: To provide language stimulation by means of visual clues.

Materials: Flannel board pieces depicting a fairy tale or cards with pictures of a fairy tale.

Directions: Tell or read aloud a story which is familiar to the students. After the story has been completed, a student is given some picture cards or flannel board pieces. These pieces or cards are to be placed in the correct order of the story. The story may be orally retold as the pieces or cards are being placed in correct order.

Variations:
1. An unfamiliar story may be read to the students who then place the cards or pieces in the order of the story.
2. Unfamiliar pictures and pieces may be presented to the students who then place them in an order and read aloud the story that the pictures tell.

4.17 Make It Like This!

Objective: To stimulate oral language development, listening comprehension, and ability to follow directions.

Materials: Clay, colored toothpicks, crayons, paint, and other available art materials.

Directions: Pair the students. One is assigned the task of thinking of an object which is to be made; the other is to make the object. The one who has the idea must orally communicate how to make the object to the other who will manipulate the art materials. The idea must not be told until after the completion of the object. At no time should the student who is giving the directions be allowed to manipulate the materials or "show" how the object should be made.

SMELL AND TASTE MODALITIES

4.18 Smell and Tell

Objective: To stimulate listening skills by creative use of the sense of smell.

Materials: Various objects which have a strong, distinguishable smell (ideally contained in small jars or containers) and a "smell" story.

> Once upon a time there was a man who grew (*pine*) trees. He grew tired of these, so he decided to grow (*orange*) trees.
> These didn't grow very well, so he tried (*coconut*) trees. These were even worse.
> His little boy asked him, "Is there such a tree as a (*vanilla*) tree?".
> "I'm afraid not," his father replied.

"How about (*chocolate*) trees?"

"No, none of those either," the father replied.

Once again the little boy tried, "How about (*peppermint*) trees?" he asked happily.

"No, sorry," the father replied. Seeing the sad look on his little boy's face, the father said, "I know just the thing!"

"I can grow (*apple*) trees!"

And so he did.

Directions: Seat the students in small groups of three or four in a circle. Place several containers nearby. Tell the story to one group at a time. As a blank in the story is reached hold the container out for the students to smell. The story continues with the students leaning forward to smell each time the story pauses. After the story has been finished the students can retell the story by supplying the words that were originally omitted. (If desired, the smells may be identified as the story is read or told.)

4.19 It Smells Like . . .

Objective: To stimulate growth in oral vocabulary by the use of the sense of smell.

Materials: Various objects to smell in small containers.

Directions: The students should be seated in a circle. Pass around an object to be smelled. Each student smells the object and states a word that describes the smell and then passes the object on. When a student cannot provide a word or whenever it is desired to use another object, the activity reverses direction.

4.20 Taste and React

Objective: To stimulate oral language development by the use of the sense of taste.

Materials: Various items to be tasted.

Directions: Give the students one item to taste or eat. Each student then orally answers questions like these:

1. It makes me feel like . . .
2. It makes me want to . . .
3. It makes me wish I could . . .
4. It makes me want to become . . .

Proceed to another student with either a similar taste or a different one.

ALPHABET

4.21 Alphabet Throw

Objective: To provide familiarity with the alphabet through kinesthetic reinforcement.

Materials: Alphabet cards, string, and large soft ball.

Directions: One letter of the alphabet is printed on each of the cards and passed out randomly. Each card has a string attached to it so that the card can be hung about the neck. The students look at their cards and then turn them over so that no one else can see them. Students then form a circle. Everyone turns their alphabet cards over so that they can be seen. Take the ball and throw it to the student who has the letter *a*. The student with letter *a* throws it to the one with letter *b*, and so on. The student with letter *z* throws it back to the teacher. If necessary, some students can have more than one alphabet card.

4.22 Piece Together the Alphabet Letter

Objective: To provide experience in the construction of the letters of the alphabet.

Materials: Various straight lines, curves, and dots made of construction paper.

Directions: Give the student a number of construction-paper lines, curves, and dots. The skill is to piece together the various letters of the alphabet.

4.23 Body Alphabet Drawing

Objective: To utilize motor modality in creating the various letters of the alphabet.

Materials: Paints, a small wading or swimming pool, a sand box, and a water box.

Directions: Tell the students to draw a letter of the alphabet using a part of the body such as a finger, a foot, or even the entire body. Where practicable the teacher also has the students draw the letter of the alphabet using all of the body parts and paints, or moving in the air (or walking), or moving in water (either waterbox for body parts, or swimming pool for entire body), or moving in sand. Some combinations are: finger—paint, move in air, move in water box, move in sand box; foot—paint, move in air, move in water box, move in sand box; and entire body—walking through the motions, moving in a swimming pool.

4.24 Children Alphabet

Objective: To utilize motor modality to reinforce the concept of the letter formations of the alphabet.

Materials: Plenty of space.

T   F

Directions: Students are divided into small groups of three to five. Assign each group a letter of the alphabet. The students should lie on the floor and curve and form their bodies together to make shapes of the letters. If the students are having difficulty with the formation, one from each group can be appointed as the director to lead the others. The director changes each time a new letter is to be made, until all have had an opportunity to be the director. The director may need to be a part of the letter, or else there may be a student who isn't needed for an occasional letter, depending on the way the children have chosen to form the letters.

LANGUAGE EXPERIENCE APPROACH

In the language experience approach, no distinction is made between the reading program and the program for developing the other language arts skills. Full development and growth in any one of these skills hinges upon full development and growth in the other skills. While the activities in this chapter—excluding the alphabet activities—fit a Language Experience Approach, this volume does not include a chapter devoted to reading activities. The language experience approach to reading is therefore briefly described here for the contributions it can make to the listening, speaking, and writing aspects of the language arts program.

This approach often begins with the development of experience charts. Experience charts are a way of preparing students for reading. But they can also prepare students for written expression, since they involve similar skills in planning what to say, organizing a logical sequence, and choosing the words to convey the intended meaning.

Experience writing is begun by the teacher with dictation from the students. This should be built around such student experiences as sensory activities, trips, activities in the classroom, letters the students dictate, science experiments, records of plans (such as plans for the day's activities), and news reports.

In working with the beginning students, the teacher can direct cooperatively developed compositions by comments and questions such as, "How shall we start? Can someone think of a better way? Do you like that way of saying it? What do we do next? How should we end? What title shall we put at the top? Have we said what we mean? Is there more that should be said? Have we put the items in the proper order?" Through such composing, students build favorable attitudes toward writing and attain practical experience in such matters as unity of subject matter, organization of thought, choice of words and phrases, and fluency of expression.

Dictation may be done individually as well as cooperatively by a small group. Sometimes a teacher may invite a pupil to think of something he or she wishes to tell and then dictate those thoughts privately. Younger students can dictate to others; parents and aides can be used as scribes. As each student talks, the teacher writes or types the dictation, placing it on a chart or on a chalkboard. The dictated composition may merit duplication and distribution for reading by the class. Stories can be bound as books and can be illustrated.

As group or individual compositions are recorded students may observe. While writing, the teacher may wish to call attention to items that are important to reading and writing, such as letter formation, association of sounds with symbols, repetition of the same sound or symbols, and the functions of capitalization and punctuation.

As soon as students express the desire to write their own compositions, they are given the opportunity to do so. As students reach an independent level in handwriting, they are provided with basic word lists. Soon they develop control over a basic vocabulary through their writing experiences. When students develop in reading ability, they are given increasing opportunities to read from books and to do more writing.

Skills grow directly out of the procedures employed to develop reading facility. Developing writing facility, in turn, makes a positive contribution to facility in word recognition, speaking, and spelling. Oral language facility increases through reading and writing by means of the dictation of stories and the discussion endemic to the storytelling process. Listening, fostered by reading good prose and poetry to the students, enables them to develop a greater sensitivity to language forms.

Some sources that provide specific activities for the above ideas include:

Allen, Roach Van, and Claryce Allen. *Language Experience Activities*. Boston: Houghton Mifflin Company, 1976.

_____ . *Language Experiences in Reading: Teachers Resource Book*. Chicago: Encyclopedia Britannica, 1966.

Hall, Mary Anne. *Teaching Reading as a Language Experience,* 3d ed. Columbus, OH: Charles E. Merrill, 1981.

Lee, Dorris M., and Richard V. Allen. *Learning to Read Through Experience*, 2d ed. Englewood Cliffs, NJ: Prentice-Hall, 1966.

Lee, Dorris, and Joseph B. Rubin. *Children and Language.* Belmont, CA: Wadsworth Publishing Company, 1979.

Stauffer, Russell G. *The Language Experience Approach to the Teaching of Reading.* New York: Harper and Row, 1970.

5 Listening

All of the language arts require listening skills. Listening largely provides the auditory discrimination, the vocabulary, and the sentence patterns that build a foundation for children to speak, read, spell, and compose. Furthermore, though many teachers are unaware of the amount of time they expect pupils to listen, practically all of the other *content areas*—history, social studies, math, science and health—require listening skills.

Teachers need to provide a proper atmosphere for listening by being a good listening model, planning well, and evaluating their oral directions. The teacher will be more effective in helping pupils to develop an appropriate listening attitude through associating listening with the many regular classroom activities, providing real purposes for listening, discussing practices that encourage better listening, and using teaching strategies that bring listening to the attention of pupils. Listening should be correlated within the entire instructional program, interwoven with the teaching of other language arts skills, and given specific attention when needed.

The teacher should utilize popular media (particularly radio and television) for improving listening and viewing skills. For example, associated with the study of television, children can be made aware of certain techniques intended to sway them toward or away from a point of view ("propaganda techniques"). Critical listening and viewing skills are necessary if listeners are to make intelligent decisions.

Listening areas in which pupils must develop competence include environmental skills, discrimination skills, and comprehension skills. Although proficiency in these skills is of major importance, interactional skills, that is an understanding of and a positive attitude toward listening, are equally important. In other words, pupils need to learn what listening is, why it is important, and how to become a good listener.

Many of the environmental skills are learned early in life, although development continues in the primary school years—such as learning that sounds differ in intensity, pitch, pattern, and duration. Discrimination skills also begin in infancy. But, as much of the primary reading program is focused upon recognizing differences in consonant sounds, vowel sounds, rhyming words, and other sound/symbol relationships, listening discrimination skills are not highlighted in this book. Comprehension skills, however, are a necessary part of the entire elementary school language arts program and will receive extensive treatment here.

A listener must be able to comprehend orally presented materials for several purposes and at several different levels. (1) *Informational listening* involves comprehending at a literal and interpretive level; understanding ideas that are directly stated is comprehension on the literal level; comprehension at the interpretive level is understanding ideas that are not directly stated but implied. (2) *Appreciative listening* involves listening for enjoyment. (3) *Analytical listening* involves comprehending at a critical and creative level; comprehension on the critical level involves evaluation of the ideas presented; on the creative listening level the listener imaginatively goes beyond the ideas actually presented.

Informational listening involves such literal and interpretive skills as:

1. Identifying stated main ideas
2. Identifying details
3. Recognizing stated cause and effect relationships
4. Detecting sequence
5. Drawing conclusions
6. Making generalizations
7. Recognizing the speaker's purpose

Appreciative listening involves such skills as:

1. Enjoying prose
2. Noting pleasing rhymes and rhythms
3. Sensing images
4. Sensing moods

Analytical listening involves such critical and creative skills as:

1. Recognizing the speaker's bias
2. Determining the speaker's qualifications
3. Determining the accuracy of the information

4. Differentiating fact from opinion
5. Recognizing propaganda techniques
6. Understanding implied cause and effect relationships
7. Visualizing the events so vividly that the listener is projected into the message
8. Using the material to solve problems
9. Predicting outcomes
10. Elaborating on what is heard

Interactional skills involve such aspects of listening as:

1. Understanding the difference between hearing and listening
2. Understanding the importance of listening
3. Understanding the responsibilities of a listener
4. Recognizing some of the factors that affect listening
5. Recognizing poor listening habits
6. Recognizing the characteristics of an effective listener

The remainder of this chapter consists of activities which can be used to teach and reinforce some of the listening skills involved in the above three aspects: environmental; comprehension (informative, appreciative, analytical); and interaction (attitudinal).

ENVIRONMENTAL SOUNDS

5.1 Sound Makers (Primary)

Objective: To use attentive listening to make students aware of the words that describe familiar sounds.

Materials: Cardboard, table, and sound making materials, such as:

two glasses (one filled with water)	triangle
rubber ball	elastic
egg beater	balloon
rhythm sticks	music box
cellophane	sand blocks

Directions: Place the above items on a table with a piece of cardboard in front of them so they cannot be seen. Ask the students to number their papers from 1 through 10. Do the following activities and have the students write beside the number the sound that they hear. (In the early school years, students may answer orally.)

Sound Makers:

1. Pour water from one glass to another.
2. Bounce a rubber ball.
3. Turn on egg beater.
4. Rub the two sand blocks together.
5. Hit the two rhythm sticks together.
6. Crinkle the cellophane.
7. Tap the triangle.
8. Pop the elastic.
9. Let the air out of a balloon slowly.
10. Play the music box.

Variation: Divide the students into pairs and have them think up sounds to use with the rest of the class.

5.2 City and Country Sounds (Primary)

Objective: To provide experience in discriminating between city and country sounds.

Materials: A bulletin board display featuring a city scene and a rural scene and a tape or record with various recorded sounds:

siren screaming	policeman's whistle
automobile horns blowing	farmer calling cows
pigs squealing	newspaper vendor calling
cricket chirping	rooster crowing
brook gurgling	dog barking

Directions: Have a group discussion of the kinds of sounds one would expect to hear in the city and also in the country. Play the tape or record for the students so that they may listen to determine which sound is a city or a country sound.

Variations:
1. Encourage students to take turns making sounds (either city or country) for their classmates to respond to.

2. On another recording, the teacher may ask students to differentiate:

> pleasant sounds and unpleasant sounds
> comforting sounds and frightening sounds
> funny sounds and sad sounds
> day sounds and night sounds
> indoor sounds and outdoor sounds
> winter sounds and summer sounds

3. Another recording can be used to differentiate sounds made by machines (car, tractor, telephone, and the like).

5.3 Associate Word and Sound (Primary)

Objective: To alert students to words associated with sounds.

Materials: A story, to be read by the teacher, which contains many opportunities for pupils to react with words that "make a sound."

Farm Sounds

Jill went to visit her grandfather's farm. She got up early when the clock ___(1)___ . She also heard a rooster ___(2)___ . Jill's grandfather was cooking breakfast. The bacon ___(3)___ , the shells of the eggs ___(4)___ , and the dry cereal ___(5)___ when Jill poured milk on it.
After breakfast, Jill and her grandfather went to feed the farm animals. The cows ___(6)___ and the pigs ___(7)___ when they were fed. The horses ___(8)___ and the sheep ___(9)___ when they saw their food.
It was a beautiful sunny day, and the birds ___(10)___ . Later in the day, Jill and her grandfather heard the dog ___(11)___ and the cat ___(12)___ . They ___(13)___ at the door because they had not been fed. Jill went to feed them, but the dog jumped up, and she spilt the food on the floor with a ___(14)___ . But the dog and cat didn't mind and ate it off the floor anyway. Jill and her grandfather ___(15)___ for a long time.

Suggested Sounds

1. rang	6. mooed	11. bark
2. cock-a-doodle-doo	7. oinked	12. meow
3. sizzled	8. whinnied	13. scratched
4. cracked	9. baaed	14. thud or crash
5. snapped or popped	10. chirped	15. giggled or laughed

Directions: Tell the students to listen carefully as the selection is being read. Advise them that you are going to stop reading at places (where the dash appears) and that you want them to supply a "sound word."

Variations:

1. Instead of supplying the word for the sound. the students may be invited to make the appropriate sound.
2. Similar stories may be developed for sounds and sound words associated with various things—city scene, machines around the home, and the like.
3. A number of poems also lend themselves to students producing the sounds mentioned in the poem. One example is "Noises at Night," by Lilian McCrea, which mentions such sounds as the train whistle, auto horns, cricket chirp, small bird peeps, and others.

INFORMATIONAL LISTENING

Literal Level Listening

5.4 Listening Detectives (Primary or Intermediate)

Objective: To provide experience in literal comprehension.

Materials: An assortment of short informational paragraphs, such as the one below:

The Great Contest

Every summer there is a wonderful event in the city of Owen. Thousands of people gather to see a great contest. It is called a hog-calling contest.

Farmers stand, shout, scream, and make "soo-ee" noises. It is hard to watch and listen to them without smiling. The best hog-caller usually wins a new tractor or farm tool. Everyone has a good time, even the hogs!

Directions: Write the words *who, what, why, when, where,* and *how* on the chalkboard to remind listeners. Tell the students to listen carefully as each selection is read. After each selection is read, ask the students to identify the *who, what, why, when, where,* and *how* facts.

Variations:
1. Several selections may be taped for listening at a listening center.
2. Students may work in pairs, with one chosen to read the passage while the other listens and identifies the facts.

5.5 What's the Idea? (Primary or Intermediate)

Objective: To help students recognize main ideas in an article read aloud.

Materials: Newspaper articles with good headlines or other passages, as suggested. (For more permanence, mount the articles on cardboard, cutting the headlines off of the articles. Put the headline on the back of the cardboard.)

> An object identified as a meteorite crashed in an unpopulated area late last night. Several citizens of a nearby town spotted the meteor as it streaked across the horizon around 11 P.M. The object was described as "a brilliant flash of light—brighter and with a longer tail than most shooting stars." The meteorite's crash created a crater six feet in depth and twelve feet in diameter.
>
> It is unusual that the rock fragment landed because as a rule objects from space burn up as they pass through the earth's atmosphere.
>
> The remaining part of the meteorite will be analyzed by the Smithsonian Institution to determine its composition and origin.

Which is the Best Headline?

The Sky Is Falling
Meteor Crashes, Crater Formed
Moon Rock Found in Field

Directions: Read the article or selection to the group. Distribute to them three possible headlines. Let them select the most appropriate one. Discuss reasons for their selections.

Variation: The same procedures may be used at a listening station, if the article or selection has been recorded. An envelope with possible headlines should accompany the taped selection.

5.6 Detail Detectives (Primary or Intermediate)

Objective: To help students locate details in a news story read aloud.

Materials: Copies of a real or a teacher-written "news story" and a list of questions about details in the story.

National Sky Show Thrills Audience

On September 21, an air show was held at the Sander Fort Air Park located just outside of Rockford, Tennessee. Parachutists representing all fifty states performed. Several of the jumpers had specially designed parachutes in different styles and shapes.

The exhibition began promptly at 9 A.M. The small airplanes left the runways and circled high overhead. Soon the first group of skydivers descended through the clouds. During their fall, they formed an eight-person circle by joining hands. Then they separated, and each floated to a perfect landing on the ground below (after opening their parachutes first of course).

The air show continued until the sun went down. Hundreds of skydivers had jumped successfully with no reported accidents. It was an event that had to be seen to be believed.

---

1. What was the occasion? (an air show)
2. Where was it held? (at the Sanders Fort Air Park)
3. Which states were represented? (all of them—fifty)
4. What type of parachutes were used? (many different ones)
5. How did the parachutists land? (perfectly)
6. What did they fall through? (the clouds)
7. How was the eight-person circle formed? (by joining hands)
8. When did the show end? (when the sun went down)
9. How many parachutists had jumped? (hundreds)
10. Were any accidents reported? (none)

Directions: Give the students the list of questions. Read aloud the news story. Ask them to answer each question after carefully listening to the article. Discuss the answers.

Interpretive Listening Level

5.7 What Might Have Happened? (Primary or Intermediate)

Objective: To provide practice in analyzing cause and effect relationships.

Materials: A trade book, library book, or basal reader.

Directions: Choose a book or story which has an obvious cause and effect situation in it. Read the entire selection or an appropriate portion of the selection to the group. Ask the students what would be the effect on the rest of the story if a certain event had not occurred or if a different event had occurred.

What If?

Mary played inside the house all day because it was raining. She left some toys scattered around the house. There was a finished puzzle at the bottom of the stairs. There were also some crayons, a doll, and a roller skate left on the stairs. Mary's father came home from work and started to walk up the stairs. Mary heard a noise and found her father lying at the bottom of the stairs.

Questions

1. What probably happened to Mary's father? (He stepped on a toy and fell down the stairs.)
2. If Mary had put away all her toys, what might have been prevented? (A fall or tripping on the stairs.)

5.8 Put It Together (Intermediate)

Objective: To provide practice in making generalizations from information that is given orally.

Materials: A set of paragraphs from which generalizations can be made and a set of questions to help lead the students to make the generalizations.

The Misunderstood Snake

There are a few living things on the face of the earth that have been misunderstood as much or as often as snakes. They actually keep very much to themselves and only fight back if they have been surprised or provoked. To some people, the mere sight of a snake is reason enough to kill it. To others, a snake means fear. What many people fail to realize is that a snake is just as afraid of a human as a human is of a snake.

Questions

1. How do some people react to snakes?
2. How do snakes actually behave?
3. What general statement can be made about a snake's behavior?

Generalization
Snakes will not harm anyone unless they are harmed themselves or threatened with harm.

Directions: Read the passage or selection to the students and ask them to answer the questions provided. Discuss with the group the reasoning behind their answers and their generalizations.

5.9 Inform, Persuade, or Entertain? (Intermediate)

Objective: To provide practice in recognizing the author's purpose.

Materials: Excerpts from material in which the author is trying to inform, persuade, or to entertain.

From the Soil to the Store (Inform)

Have you ever walked into a store and bought some vegetables and wondered where they came from? It takes months for a farmer to grow the tomatoes, potatoes, and the beans that you buy at a store. First, the farmer has to prepare the soil by plowing and tilling. Fertilizer is then spread on the ground so the seeds will get enough nutrients. After this, the farmer makes rows in which to plant the seeds. After the seeds are planted, the farmer then covers the seeds. During the months ahead, the farmer must keep the ground watered and keep the weeds away. When the vegetables begin to ripen, then the farmer begins to harvest them. Sometimes farmers pick them by hand; sometimes farmers use equipment which can gather the vegetables faster. After harvest, the farmer delivers the vegetables to the store where they are cleaned and prepared for the shopper to use.

Don't You Want This Pen? (Persuade)

Todd's pen ran out of ink while taking a test one day in class. Todd complained by saying, "I only bought the pen two days ago and it's already out of ink." Brad told him about a pen which was better.

Brad said, "My pen has enough ink to last me for at least six months. It's also guaranteed not to run out of ink during that time. If it does, I get my money back. I like my pen better because it also erases when I make a mistake." Todd was so convinced that he went to the nearest store and bought one. The next day, Todd thanked Brad for telling him about the pen. Todd said, "Now I'll never have to worry about my pen running out of ink during a test. After all, I want the best when taking a test."

A Night at the Fights (Entertain)

Jim and John went to the wrestling matches one night. A big crowd gathered to watch their favorite wrestlers meet their opponents. Jim cheered as one of the wrestlers flew through the air to tackle his opponent. John laughed as the fans booed the bad wrestlers who choked their opponents or pulled their opponent's hair. When their favorite wrestlers pinned their opponents, Jim and John cheered. Jim and John enjoyed watching the wrestlers and the fans. Jim and John want to go to another "night at the fights."

Directions: Read each selection aloud. Ask the students to classify them according to the author's purpose by writing the appropriate word by the number (order) of the selections read. After the students have completed their work, discuss the reasons for their classifications.

APPRECIATIVE LISTENING

5.10 Draw a Poem! (Primary or Intermediate, depending upon level of poem)

Objective: To provide an opportunity for students to respond to poems through drawing or painting a picture.

Materials: A collection of "visual" poems, such as the following:

Rachel Field	*Dorothy Aldis*
"Skyscraper"	"Windy Washing Day"
"Taxis"	"Hiding"
"General Store"	
"Roads"	

Robert Louis Stevenson   *Eleanor Farjeon*
"My Shadow"   "The Sounds in the Morning"
"Black City"

Directions: Read aloud a selected poem. Then instruct the students to make a drawing to represent the poem.

Variations:
1. See Activity 4.16 for another idea.
2. For a number of appreciative listening activities, see D. and E. Russell's *Listening Aids Through the Grades*. New York: Columbia University Press, 1979.

ANALYTICAL LISTENING

Critical Listening Level

5.11 Bias Detectives (Intermediate)

Objective: To provide practice in recognizing the effect an author's bias may have on his or her speaking or writing.

Materials: Two articles on the same subject written by authors who have opposing political, religious, or other beliefs.

The Idea of Communism

In its original form, communism is an ideal thought. When Karl Marx wrote *The Communist Manifesto* in 1848, he saw a large group of workers who were being taken advantage of by their bosses, the capitalists. From this, he predicted conflict between the working class (proletariat) and the ruling class (bourgeoisie). Marx based this idea on both historical and contemporary events. The resulting revolution would leave a class of workers who would reject the idea of private property so that all would have equal shares. Marx's idea of communism was best expressed in his statement, "From each according to his ability, to each according to his need."

The System of Capitalism

For the majority of Americans, capitalism is the best system for economic growth. As Adam Smith wrote in his *The Wealth of Nations* in 1776, an open market system that is free of control will take care of itself. The system is founded on the idea that demand for a product will determine its production, supply, and price. Smith also saw that such a system will bring financial growth to the society that uses it. By using a division of labor where each worker has a specialized job, more products can be produced. Together, this system continues to work well and create jobs and wages for the large labor force that make up this country.

Directions: Tell the students that you have two articles written by two authors who have opposing beliefs. Name the topic and if possible give the students some pertinent background information about each of the authors. Ask questions such as, "Will these two authors feel the same way about the topic? Do you think the way they feel will influence their ideas? In what way? What kinds of things do you expect Author One to say? What kinds of things do you expect Author Two to say?"

After these points have been discussed, read the articles to the students. Follow the reading with a discussion of the accuracy of the students' predictions about what the authors would say. Bring out any evidences of bias in the articles. This activity will work most effectively when the articles represent views on a currently controversial issue that is relevant to the students' lives and interests.

5.12 Propaganda Hunt (Intermediate)

Objective: To foster analytical listening (and viewing) skills for television.

Materials: Boxes with the names of seven propaganda techniques on them, as:

Name calling	Glittering generalities
Transfer technique	Plain folks talk
Testimonial technique	Bandwagon technique
	Card stacking

Directions: Previous to this activity, the students should learn the propaganda techniques. Discuss definitions and examples of the various propaganda techniques.

1. Name Calling—use of negative labels toward a person: "Bill is 'yellow.'"
2. Glittering Generalities—use of vague words to "sell" an idea: "He trusts us; let's trust him with our vote."
3. Transfer Technique—association of a respected symbol with a person or thing: "This racquet is used by the top tennis player in the world."
4. Plain Folks Talk—relation of a person to the common people: "He is one of us working-class laborers."
5. Testimonial Technique—use of a popular person to endorse product or proposal: "Miss Movie Star says: I use Shiny Toothpaste. Why don't you?"
6. Bandwagon Technique—use of the idea that "everyone" is doing a particular activity: "Everyone is buying one. Get yours today!"
7. Card Stacking—revealing one side of a story only: "This is the best buy—it is larger." (But it is also much more expensive and not well made.)

Have students find examples of these techniques in television commercials and describe the examples, placing them in the appropriate boxes. As a group activity, each example can be evaluated for its appropriateness for the category in which it was placed.

Creative Listening Level

5.13 Word Pictures (Primary or Intermediate)

Objective: To provide practice in visualizing scenes and situations presented in written form.

Materials: A copy of a set of paragraphs that vividly describe scenes or situations. Pencils and crayons. Drawing paper.

The Secret Door

Jeff stood in front of the big wooden door and slowly turned the doorknob. As the door opened, Jeff saw many brightly colored things inside the room. His mouth opened in surprise. The room was filled with toys! There were red and yellow balls, polka dotted jack-in-the-boxes, shiny silver play guns, and big stuffed animals. Hundreds of other toys were all around the room. Jeff had never seen so many toys in his life.

Directions: Read one paragraph. Distribute the drawing paper and the pencils and crayons to the students. Instruct them to illustrate the scene or situation described in the paragraph. When the students have finished, let them share their pictures and see how different people visualized the same scene differently.

5.14 What Would You Have Done? (Intermediate)

Objective: To foster the idea that some stories offer possible solutions to problems.

Materials: A book or story in which a problem is solved.
Overcoming Handicaps
Davidson, Margaret. *Helen Keller.* New York: Hasting House, 1969; (blind and deaf).
Lasker, Joe. *He's My Brother.* Chicago: Whitman, 1974; (learning disability).
Family Situations
Blume, Judy. *It's Not the End of the World.* New York: Bradbury, 1972; (divorce).
Caine, Jeannette. *Abby.* New York: Harper, 1973; (adoption).
Understanding Emotions
Lee, Virginia. *The Magic Moth.* New York: Seabury Press, 1972; (death).
Rolerson, Darrell A. *A Boy Called Plum.* New York: Dodd, 1974; (loneliness).
Social Concerns
Clifton, Lucille. *Good, Says Jerome.* New York: Dutton, 1973; (making friends).
Konigsburg, E.L. *The Dragon in the Ghetto Caper.* New York: Atheneum, 1974; (crime).

Directions: Read the book or story to the students. Let them discuss these questions:

1. What problem did the character(s) in the story face?
2. How was the problem handled?

3. Was the solution a good one?
4. What other solutions might have been found?
5. Would these solutions have been better or worse than the solution presented in the story?

5.15 Add Some More (Intermediate)

Objective: To encourage students to imagine events beyond the stories they have heard.

Materials: Appropriate books or stories, such as

Eager, Edward. *Half Magic* in Edna Johnson's *Anthology of Children's Literature*. Boston: Houghton Mifflin, 1959, pp. 652–663.

Enright, Elizabeth. *The Saturdays*. New York: Dell Publishing Co., 1966.

Holling, C.H. *Paddle to the Sea*. Boston: Houghton Mifflin, 1941.

Lewis, C.S. *The Lion, the Witch, and the Wardrobe*. New York: Macmillan, 1950.

Lindgren, Astrid. *Pippi Longstocking*. New York: Viking, 1950.

Norton, Mary. *The Magic Bed-Knob* in M.H. Arbuthnot, *The Arbuthnot Anthology of Children's Literature: Time for Fairy Tales*. Chicago: Scott, Foresman, 1961, p. 326.

Directions: Ask students to write another episode to the book or story that is read aloud to them, using the characters and settings from the story. These episodes can be shared orally in small groups.

INTERACTIONAL SKILLS

5.16 Simon Says (Primary)

Objective: To provide practice in attentive listening.

Materials: Set of directions to be used alternatively with and without "Simon Says."

Directions: The students stand in a circle. The teacher or a classmate acts as the leader and gives directions to the group. The students follow only the directions which are prefaced by the phrase "Simon Says" but are "out" if they follow directions which are not so prefaced. The last one to remain standing is the winner of the game.

5.17 Listen and Do (Primary)

Objective: To help the student better understand the importance of listening.

Materials: Copy of sheet as suggested below, pencil, and crayons.

1	2	3
4	5	6
7	8	9

Directions: Hand out sheets. Tell students that you will read directions, telling them what to draw in each square. Explain that the directions will be read only once. Read the directions, as

Make a blue circle in box 6.
Make a green and yellow ball in box 8.
Make a red hat in box 5.
Make a green and brown tree in box 2.
Put your name in box 1.
Make a blue triangle in box 7.
Make 3 black stripes in box 4.
Make a green circle in box 9.
Make a yellow square in box 3.

Let students check their own papers with a correct model.

Variations:
1. Let a student give the directions to another student or the group of students.
2. Let different students make up their own directions.

5.18 Graph Puzzle (Intermediate)

Objective: To help students appreciate the importance of listening.

Materials: Copy of graph puzzle as illustrated below and crayons.

GRAPH PUZZLE

	1	2	3	4	5	6	7	8	9
A									
B									
C									
D									
E									

Directions: Hand out the sheets. Tell the students you will read directions once, telling them which squares to color. If they follow directions correctly, they will find the message HI. Read the directions as follows: Color D 2; B 8; C 3; D 8; B 2; C 7; B 6; D 4; B 7; C 2; B 4; D 6; C 4; D 7.

Variations:
1. Let a student give the directions to another student or the group of students.
2. Let different students make up their own directions for such a graph puzzle.

5.19 Listen—and Help Tell the Story (Primary)

Objective: To demonstrate the need for attentive listening in a group activity.

Materials: A ball of yarn which has been previously unwound, had knots tied at intervals of every few feet, and rewound. A "tall tale" or other story with which the students are familiar.

Directions: The group should sit in a circle. The teacher begins to tell a story such as Paul Bunyan or another familiar narrative. The teacher unwinds the yarn while talking. When the teacher comes to a knot, the yarn is passed to the student on the right. This student continues the story until reaching a knot, then passes it on. The story may continue as long as time and yarn permits. If the yarn runs out, simply rewind it and start again.

6 Oral Composition

Why is it important to teach oral composition to elementary school students? Most children can communicate orally by the time they come to school, but there is a genuine need to develop oral *fluency* (a willingness to use language), to further syntactic and vocabulary development, and to prompt creative self-expression.

As oral composition activities are being presented, the teacher may be assured that the enjoyment and excitement which the students are displaying does not mean that they are not learning. Quite the contrary, the students are actually learning how to listen better, to write creatively, to organize and place ideas in sequence, to read better, and to build their vocabularies. As oral language is the "parent" of all the other language arts, learning how to speak more fluently benefits all of the language skills in a mutually reinforcing manner.

The role of the teacher involves more than presenting the needed information about oral expression to the students. The teacher must help students to use their ongoing experiences as occasions for oral language expression and create other experiences which will facilitate language learning and expression. These experiences should involve the content areas as well as the language period. Students will thus *use* language instead of merely "doing language." The teacher is also responsible for providing a positive *environment* for encouraging the free use of oral expression. The students in a classroom must have the opportunity to talk freely among themselves and with the teacher without fear of punishment. The environment should be flexible; students should not remain seated in the same place in the classroom and in vertical rows for long periods of time. Many other classroom seating arrangements are more suitable for stimulating oral expression—circle and semi-circle arrangements especially. The best seating arrangement, however, is the one which is best suited for the specific activity.

Perhaps the most important element in providing an atmosphere conducive to total language development is a classroom free of emotional stress, threat, or fear. The student who is fearful will not be willing to express the inner thoughts which need to be spoken. With a positive, supportive, and concern-filled classroom, though, even the most timid students will express themselves orally, and the teacher will have the added joy not only of stimulating that student's language development but also of reaching to the very heart of the student and touching a life. (Needless to add, the teacher must provide an acceptable model for speaking.)

Four major avenues for enhancing oral expression are developed within this chapter: storytelling, drama, general oral activities, and describing and discussing.

When teaching the art of storytelling to students, or when telling a story to the class, there are several guidelines which will help assure the listeners of a well-told story. The story which is to be shared should be very real to the teller, whether it is an actual experience, a short story, or an original idea. The storyteller should be so familiar with the story and all its details that there is little possibility of forgetting. It is also helpful for the storyteller to remember some of the original vocabulary, in order to create mood and atmosphere and to convey emotion. All the knowledge, skills, and talent of the storyteller should be used to tell the story simply, directly, and with complete ease and freedom. The storyteller should also use pacing appropriately, varying the speed of the story and using pauses to accentuate points of climax. The teller should use all the potentials of the voice, varying pitch for different characters and for different moods, working for appropriate strength and resonance. The teller needs to develop good rapport with the listeners in order to create for them and with them a living experience. Lastly, the storyteller can often enhance the story by utilizing appropriate media to heighten the effects. Some stories lend themselves to the flannel board, others to puppets, and still others to props (such as preparing "stone soup" while telling the story of the same name by Marcia Brown). The activities in the first part of this chapter focus upon helping students to compose a sequential story, to sense the major parts of a story, and to use varied techniques while storytelling.

Drama has a number of possibilities for the development of oral language skills. Some major categories of drama include choral drama, sociodrama (role-playing), creative dramatics, scripted plays, and puppetry. Many teachers find the use of echoic verse a good introduction to other forms of choral reading. With echoic verse, the teacher or reader speaks a line and the audience echos it, word for word, intonation for intonation. Only the reader has a copy of the verse. All students can participate, since no reading is involved, and can focus upon the thought and expression of the verse. Choral drama involves dramatic lines being spoken by groups in unison or other arrangements. An interesting way to supplement the pleasure of choral drama is to have one group of students speak the choral parts while another group pantomimes the other spoken parts. Sociodrama involves confronting the students with a problem; they then temporarily put their own identity aside and act out the problem. The ultimate goal is for a solution to the problem to develop spontaneously. Creative dramatics includes a variety of activities, including impromptu plays, acting out situations in stories, and improvising drama. The process involved in creative dramatics includes sharpening the sense and sensitivity, becoming aware of the power and meaning of motion, becoming a character, and acting impromptu and creatively with no script. Scripted plays are formalized plays with parts, a cast, and staging, all requiring varying amounts of preparation. Puppetry may be any of the other types of dramatic play with the addition of puppets as visual props. An interesting variation of puppetry is the use of silhouettes (shadowplay cast on a white background) instead of the traditional puppets or marionettes. The activities in the second part of this chapter include a sociodrama situation, debate drama, role playing, creative improvisation, echoic and choral speaking.

In addition to storytelling and drama, a great number of general oral language activities can be used to develop specific skills of oral expression. The first four activities in the third section "More Talk" are intended to draw attention to words that may be used in speaking situations. The last four activities focus upon four specific speaking situations: humorous items, description, comparison and evaluation, and discussion. (See Subject-Skill Index of Activities for other oral expression activities—choral speaking, drama, oral expression, pantomime, puppetry, storytelling.)

STORYTELLING

6.1 Story Darts (Primary or Intermediate)

Objective: To provide familiarity with the concept of story sequence.

Materials: A dart board (with lifting or removable panels, made of poster board or similar type material), safety darts (either commercial rubber-tipped darts or "home made" of small rods with masking tape, sticky side out, stuck to the ends), and a set of pictures pasted behind each dart panel.

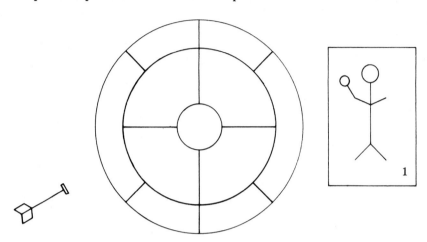

Directions: Behind each panel of the dartboard place a numbered picture of a segment of a story sequence, such as a frame of a cartoon strip. When a student throws a dart the panel is lifted, revealing the numbered picture frame. The next student throws a dart and lifts another panel, revealing another numbered picture of a segment of the comic strip or story. Play continues until all the panels have been removed. Then the group arranges the pictures in order and each student tells his or her part of the story.

Variation: Wordless (textless) books with pictures may be used to elicit storytelling and the concept of story sequence. Here are some titles:

Anno, Mitsumasa. *Topsy-Turvies: Pictures to Stretch the Imagination.* Weatherhill, 1970. (See sequel *Upside-Downers: More Pictures to Stretch the Imagination.* Weatherhill, 1971; also see *Anno's Journey.* Cleveland: Collins World, 1978.)

Barton, Byron. *Harry Is a Scaredy-Cat.* New York: Macmillan, 1974.

Briggs, Raymond. *The Snowman.* New York: Random House, 1978.

Carle, Eric. *Do You Want to Be My Friend?* New York: Crowell, 1971.

―――. *I See a Song.* New York: Crowell, 1973.

Carroll, Ruth. *Chimp and the Clown.* New York: Walch, 1968. (See others by Carroll, same publisher: *Rolling Downhill,* 1973; *The Dolphin and the Mermaid.* 1974.)

DeGroat, Diane. *Alligator's Toothache.* New York: Crown Publishers, 1977.

De Paola, Tomie. *Pancakes for Breakfast*. New York: Macmillan, 1972.

Freeman, Don. *The Chalk Box Story*. Philadelphia: Lippincott, 1976.

Fromm, Lilo. *Muffel and Plums*. New York: Macmillan, 1972.

*Goodall, John S. *The Surprise Picnic*. New York: Atheneum, 1977. (Also see by the same author: *An Edwardian Summer*. Atheneum, 1976; *Paddy Pork's Holiday*. Atheneum, 1976; *Naughty Nancy*. Atheneum, 1975; *Jackco*. Harcourt, 1972; *Paddy's Evening Out*. Atheneum, 1973; *Shrewbettina's Birthday*. Harcourt, 1971; *The Story of An English Village*. Atheneum, 1978.)

Hartelius, Margaret. *The Chicken's Child*. New York: Doubleday, 1975.

Hogrogian, Nonny. *Apples*. New York: Macmillan, 1972.

Hom, Jesper, and Sven Gronlyke. *For Kids Only*. New York: Delacorte, 1977.

Hutchines, Pat. *Changes, Changes*. New York: Macmillan, 1971.

Keats, Jack. *The Egg Book*. New York: Macmillan, 1975.

*Krahn, Fernando. *A Funny Friend from Heaven*. Philadelphia: Lippincott, 1977. (Also see by same author: *April Fools*. New York: Dutton, 1974; *The Mystery of the Giant's Footprints*. Dutton, 1977; *Who's Seen the Scissors*. Dutton, 1975.)

Mayer, Mercer. *The Great Cat Chase: A Wordless Book*. New York: Four Winds, 1975. (Also see by same author *Two Moral Tales*, 1974; *One Frog Two Many*, 1975; *Bubble Bubble*. Parents Magazine Press, 1973; *A Boy, A Dog and A Friend*. New York: Parents Magazine Press, 1973; *Frog Goes to Dinner*. New York: Dial, 1974; *Frog on His Own*. New York: Dial, 1973; *Frog Where Are You?* New York: Dial, 1969.)

*Mendoza, George. *The Inspector*. New York: Doubleday, 1970.

Peppe, Rodney. *Humpty Dumpty*. New York: Viking, 1976.

Turkle, Brinton. *Deep in the Forest*. New York: Dutton, 1976.

Ueno, Noriko. *Elephant Buttons*. New York: Harper, 1973.

*Ward, Lund K. *The Silver Pony: A Story in Pictures*. Boston: Houghton Mifflin, 1973.

Winter, Paul. *The Bear and the Fly*. New York: Crown Publishers, 1976.

*Appropriate for upper primary/early intermediate levels.

6.2 Play the Story Game Board (Intermediate)

Objective: To provide experience in composing a story sequentially.

Materials: A game board with story cues written on the spaces and a coin.

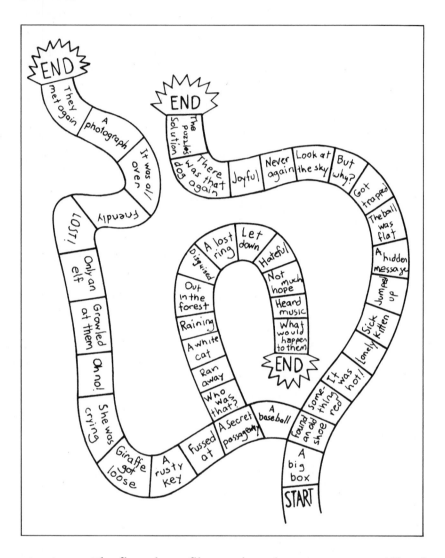

Directions: The first player flips a coin and moves one space if heads and two spaces if tails. On the first move, Player One begins a story using the cue from the space on the game board. Allow a minute or so for that portion of the story. Player Two then flips the coin, moves accordingly, and continues the story using the cue from the space landed upon. Allow a set amount of time for each student's part of the story. Play continues until each player comes to "End."

Variation: For younger students, instead of word cues, pictures may be used in the board's spaces.

6.3 Start, Continue, Climax, and Finish! (Intermediate)

Objective: To familiarize students with the structures of storytelling.

Materials: Index cards with story "starters," "continuers," "climaxes," and "finishers" written on them, in four separate file card boxes: Box 1: Story Starters; Box 2: Story Continuers; Box 3: Story Climaxes; Box 4: Story Finishers.

Box 1

"There once was an old woman who lived in a velvet green forest. While she was cleaning out her barn one lonely, drizzling day, she found an egg, the likes of which she had never before seen!"	"Have you ever heard the story of why dragons breathe fire and brimstone? Well, let me tell you. . ."	"I'd never heard singing like that before! What was that exquisite song, coming forth so gently, as if from the very ground?"

Box 2

"That old guinea pig jumped and squirmed and tried its best to get away. What a noise it made when it squealed!"	"No, please don't make me go out there again!"	"Well, anyway, the boy decided that they couldn't keep on going. Something was going to have to happen, but he was determined it wasn't going to be him or his friends who were caught."

Box 3

"The cloud of flame whirled and spun until it finally exploded into thousands of scorching, burning colors."	"There was no hope left for them. They had just resolved to accept their impossible fate. But just then. . ."	"You should have seen her! She was so puffed up and twisted out of shape you couldn't even recognize her for the true beauty she was. . ."

Box 4

"Some dreams just never do end but keep on going and going. . ."	"Do you think they all lived happily ever after? Well, let me just tell you how it was. . ."	"I often wonder why things have to happen the way they do. But at least we can say. . ."

Directions: The student randomly draws a card from each box and reads silently. When the student is ready (approximately five minutes), the oral storytelling can begin. The story should include each of the segments on the cards which were drawn.

Variations:
1. For younger students paste pictures on the cards to be drawn.
2. This activity can be done as a creative writing assignment.

6.4 Tell It Creatively (Primary or Intermediate)

Objective: To promote creative expression in storytelling.

Materials: Supply of trade books and a bulletin board display as follows.

Name of Book	Idea for Sharing
1. *Jennie's Hat* by Keats	Decorate hat with various items as the story is told
2. *Book of Fairy Tales* by Tudor	Use hand puppets
3. *Harold and Purple Crayon* by Johnson	Make a chalk talk as Harold did
4. *The Little Woman Wanted Noise* by Teal	Provide sound effects as the story is told
5. *The Three Pigs* by Izawa	Provide appropriate background music for the pigs and the wolf
6. *The Happy Owls* by Piatti	Use paper folding (Origami: See John Montroll. *Origami for the Enthusiast: Step by Step Instruction in Over 700 Diagrams.* New York: Dover, 1980.)

Directions: The teacher should tell the students that there are a variety of ways to tell stories. Taking *Jennie's Hat* as an example. The teacher tells the story with a hat in hand. As the story is told, the hat is decorated with various items as suggested by the story (flowers, feathers, ribbons, leaves, etc.).

The teacher should continue to illustrate, on numerous occasions, a variety of ways to tell stories. Gradually, students can be encouraged to utilize various means of enriching their storytelling. At times, small groups may plan together to tell a story in an original manner. The type of presentation is dependent upon the particular story chosen.

DRAMA

6.5 Act and Talk It Out! (Primary or Intermediate)

Objective: To provide the opportunity to orally create solutions to problems.

Materials: 5″ × 8″ file cards with problems, mysteries, or dilemmas, printed on them.

> Your mother and your friend's mother are at a luncheon party. So you and your friend go exploring in the woods. After you have been wandering for over an hour you realize you should be getting back. But you also realize that you're lost. What will you do?

> You are late to class and there is a spelling test awaiting you. Then, there before you is a puppy that has broken a leg. You look around and see no one. What will you do?

> While Christmas shopping, your friend slips a deck of cards into her or his pocket from the counter. She or he thinks you didn't see. What will you do?

Directions: Pass the file cards out one at a time. After time for consideration of the situation, students are to act out the situation. It is assumed that a "warm-up" under teacher direction will be provided, with full discussion of the situation by class members.

Variation: Allow the students to discuss among themselves how they will solve the dilemma. Then have the students act out the solution.

6.6 Fussy Puppets (Intermediate)

Objective: To provide an opportunity to debate.

Materials: Various puppets and a puppet theater (stage). (The puppet theater should have movable lecterns where the debating puppets can stand.)

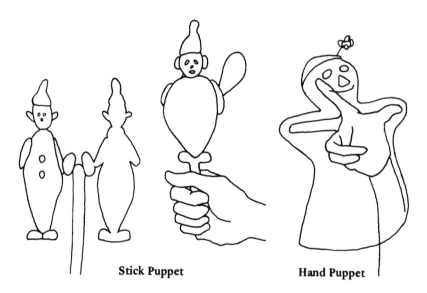

Stick Puppet   **Hand Puppet**

Directions: Two puppets are selected to debate a topic that is totally worthless—why dogs should or should not be taught to blow bubbles with bubble gum, for example. After receiving the topic for debate, the puppeteers are allowed fifteen minutes for preparation. The debate should be conducted orderly by a moderator (the teacher or another pupil) to include time for presentation of points and rebuttals by each puppet.

Variation: See such valuable references about puppetry as the following:

Cummings, Richard. *101 Hand Puppets*. New York: David McKay, 1962.

Gated, Frieda. *Easy to Make Puppets*. New York: Harvey House Publishers, 1976.

Lewis, Shari. *Making Easy Puppets*. New York: E.P. Dutton, 1967.

Mahlmann, Lewis, and David C. Jones. *Puppet Plays for Young Players*. Boston: Plays, Inc., 1974.

Ross, Laura. *Hand Puppets—How to Make and Use Them*. New York: Lothrop, Lee and Shepard, 1969.

——. *Finger Puppets—Easy to Make, Fun to Use*. New York: Lothrop, Lee and Shepard, 1971.

6.7 Be the Character (Intermediate)

Objective: To provide experiences in characterization.

Materials: Index cards with selected discussion topics and characters printed on cards.

Topic	*Characters*
1. I am afraid of you.	An elephant and a mouse
2. How to conserve space.	A lunchbox and a thermos jug
3. How to be compatible friends.	A porcupine and an armadillo
4. How to sound good together.	A tuba and a piccolo
5. How to get along better.	A goat and a pig
6. How we will take care of each other.	A tree and a flower
7. What can we do about this robbery?	The knife and gun of a thief
8. Let's compromise.	A beaver and a stream
9. You are my best friend.	A boy or girl and a dog

Directions: Have the students pair off. Each pair randomly selects a discussion topic and assumes the role of one of the characters. They then begin discussing the topics as if they were the characters.

Variation: Students can write out dialogue between characters, which they then can act out themselves.

6.8 Matter of Perspective (Intermediate)

Objective: To stimulate the creative description of characters or objects.

Materials: Index cards with selected characters or objects printed on cards.

1. A black pearl still in an oyster
2. A seasick pirate
3. An old, blind horse
4. A ferris wheel
5. A maple leaf
6. A cigarette
7. A new nickel
8. An orphaned wolf cub
9. A rose
10. A wheelchair
11. A telegram
12. A Get Well card
13. A key
14. A used toothpick
15. An old trumpet
16. A tennis ball
17. A broken pair of glasses
18. A wasp's nest
19. An old lady's shawl
20. An Antebellum colonial mansion

Directions: Each student selects or randomly picks a character or object and then tells what it is like being that character. Answers to questions such as suggested should also be included in the descriptions. These may be written on the chalkboard or posted on the bulletin board as "reminders."

1. How did you get to be like you are?
2. What is your life like?
3. Would you recommend others to share your life? Why or why not?
4. Are you happy? Why or why not?
5. How do people treat you?
6. How would you describe yourself?
7. What do you think your future will be like?
8. Tell about the most interesting/happy/dangerous/sad experience you've ever had.
9. What is the meaning of your life?
10. What advice would you like to give me?

Variation: This activity may also be used as a creative writing activity.

6.9 Echo! Echo! (Primary)

Objective: To provide experience in speaking clearly and expressively.

Materials: Poems which lend themselves to echoic reading such as "The Little Turtle" and "The Mysterious Cat" by Vachel Lindsay, "The Night Will Never Stay" by Eleanor Farjeon, "The Goat" (anonymous), and "To Market, To Market" (Mother Goose).

Directions: Explain echoic verse: the reader says a line and the audience repeats it, word for word, intonation for intonation, and sometimes even action for action. Then lead the students through a poem or tale. Students themselves can then take turns leading the echoic reading.

6.10 Say It in Different Ways (Intermediate)

Objective: To provide practice with choral reading in various arrangements.

Materials: A verse that lends itself to speaking as follows:

Monday's child is fair of face,
Tuesday's child is full of grace,
Wednesday's child is full of woe,
Thursday's child has far to go,
Friday's child is loving and giving,
Saturday's child works for its living,
And a child that is born on the Sabbath is fair and wise and good and gay.

Directions: A group of six students may wish to study together for the speaking of this verse. Important words which will be emphasized in each line may be underlined, such as *"Monday's* child is *fair* of *face* . . ."* A tape recorder may be helpful for practice before sharing with a larger group of peers.

After presenting it as illustrated, the group may wish to use these variations.

1. *Line-a-child* or *line-a-group.* Each student (or group) reads at least one line as a solo. Some lines may be spoken in unison.
2. *Refrain or chorus.* One student speaks a solo part and a group reads the refrain or chorus.
3. *Two-part or antiphonal.* Two groups of students take turn speaking the lines.
4. *Unison.* All groups may say together the same lines.

Variations:

1. Other refrain types of choral reading may be utilized ("The Wind" by Robert Louis Stevenson for primary years; "Shoes and Stockings" by A. A. Milne for the intermediate years), or line-a-child readings ("The Goblin" by Rose Fyleman for the primary years and "Pippa's Song" by Robert Browning for the intermediate years).
2. Try unison choral reading with "Poor Old Woman" and "Trains" by James Tippett for the primary years; "Roads" by Rachel Fields and "Jonathan Bing" by Beatrice Brown for the intermediate years.
3. See also such sources of choral reading as May Hill Arbuthnot and Shelton Root, *Time for Poetry* (Glenview, IL: Scott, Foresman and Company, 1968); and Marjory F. Brown-Azarowicz, *A Handbook of Creative Choral Speaking* (Minneapolis, MN: Burgess, 1970).

MORE TALK

6.11 Don't Stop Talking (Primary)

Objective: To help students gain fluency and ease in speaking.

Materials: An egg-timer.

Directions: As soon as the timer is started the student must begin talking about any subject or about a preselected topic until the time has run out.

6.12 Circle Sound-a-Rhyme (Primary)

Objective: To increase students' awareness of rhyme.

Materials: Sample list of sounds.

-at	-op	-ee	-ick
-it	-ip	-oo	-ug
-ot	-ap	-or	-ill

Directions: Seat students in a circle. Proceed around the circle with each student saying a word that rhymes with the given sound. Play begins on the next sound when no one can think of additional rhyming words.

6.13 Roll-a-Sound (Primary or Intermediate)

Objective: To provide practice in producing words with given consonants.

Materials: Four large six-faced cubes constructed of poster board. One die (or a poster-board cube with numerals 1 through 6 written on the six faces).

Directions: Write the twenty-one consonants on the cubes. The three additional spaces should have "Choice" written on them. Play begins with a student taking a consonant cube and rolling it and then rolling the numeral die. The student must then say as many words as the numeral shows; the words must all begin with the consonant shown on the consonant cube.

Variations:
1. The consonant cube that is rolled may be an ending or medial consonant in the words produced.
2. The student may roll two consonant cubes and provide words containing both consonant sounds. Advanced students can try it with three or more cubes as a challenge.
3. Without using the number die, the student may say as many words beginning (or ending) with the consonant shown on the consonant cube. For each word spoken the student receives one point and continues saying words for thirty seconds. Play continues until someone reaches a designated number of points.

6.14 The Give-Gave Game (Primary)

Objective: To provide practice in forming verb tenses.

Materials: Ball or other object.

Directions: A ball or other object is given to a student, who passes it on to three other students. The player then tells to whom it has been given and asks for its return. Example: "I gave the ball to

May. May gave it to Sue. Sue gave it to John. John may give it to me." Then play resumes with the player first given the ball.

Variations:

1. If memory is a problem, the ball or other object may be given to only one or two students. To extend memory, the ball or object may be given to four or more students before being returned to the original possessor.
2. Many other usage situations lend themselves to such games. For example, "haven't any." The game is started by a student making the statement, "I haven't any _____ ." Another pupil answers with the same statement and supplies a rhyming last word, as "I haven't any books. I haven't any hooks."

SOME SPEAKING SITUATIONS

6.15 Joking Around (Primary)

Objective: To provide an opportunity to have fun with language.

Materials: Enough knock-knock jokes, riddles, two-part jokes or puns, or tongue-twisters for every student in the class. The jokes should be printed on index cards and inserted in envelopes as shown.

Envelope 1

Half 1-Joke 1	"What's the difference between a cat and a semicolon?"
Half 2-Joke 2	"A sun-burned penguin."

Envelope 2

Half 1-Joke 2	"What's black, white and red all over?"
Half 2-Joke 1	"A cat has claws at the end of its paws; a semicolon has a pause at the end of its clause!"

Directions:

1. Write on separate cards the two parts of the joke.
2. Put in envelopes the initial part of one joke and the finishing part of another joke.
3. Each student then receives an envelope.
4. Every student then goes around the room asking their jokes to each other to see if that person has the last half of their

joke. In turn, they are being asked jokes also, to see if they have the last half of another person's joke.

5. When two students find their jokes match they lock arms and continue searching for the remaining joke halves.

6. The envelopes should contain joke halves in such a manner that the students ultimately join arms to form a circle. (Note: *no* numbers should appear on the envelopes or the joke since these might be clues as to how the joke halves fit together.)

7. After the students have formed a circle (they may reverse arms with their partners if it is necessary), they are then told to sit on the floor in the circle.

8. Each student may then share their joke with the rest of the group, going around the circle answering and responding.

Variations:

1. Students may create their own jokes to be used.

2. See such sources as the following for jokes, riddles, poems, or tongue-twisters:

Boys' Life. The Best Jokes from Boys' Life. New York: Putnam's Sons, 1970.

Bridwell, Norman. *Monster Jokes and Riddles*. New York: Scholastic Book Services, 1972.

Cole, William. *The Square Bear and Other Riddle Rhymers*. New York: Scholastic Book Services, 1976.

Doty, Roy. *Q's are Weird O's: More Puns, Gags, Quips, and Riddles*. Garden City, NY: Doubleday, 1975.

Emrich, Duncan. *Riddles and Jokes and Foolish Facts*. New York: Scholastic Book Services, 1972.

Ridlon, Marci. *A Frog Sandwich: Riddles and Jokes*. Chicago: Follett Publishing Co., 1973.

Schwartz, Alvin. *A Twister of Twists, a Tangler of Tongues*. Philadelphia: Lippincott, 1972.

———. *Witcracks—Jokes and Jest from American Folklore*. Philadelphia: Lippincott, 1972.

———. *Tom Foolery—Trickery and Foolery with Words*. Philadelphia: Lippincott, 1973.

Thaler, Miles. *Magic Letter Riddles*. New York: Scholastic Book Services, 1974.

6.16 Describe, Compare, Evaluate (Primary)

Objective: To provide student experiences with describing, comparing, and evaluating.

Materials: Actual objects as suggested below or pictures of paired objects, as

    a fireman's hat—a policeman's hat
    a baseball game—a concert
    a dog—a cat
    a fountain pen—a magic marker
    a piano—an organ
    a school building—a church building
    a triangle—a square
    a jacket—a sweater
    a radio—a television set
    a book—a magazine
    a basketball—a football

Directions: The class is led in discussion of what makes objects alike or different. Topics would include such features as color, shape, size, weight, texture, use, temperature, aroma, and taste. Students, with three to five to a group, select several paired items. They are asked to talk about how they are alike and how they are different. After consulting among themselves they are to arrive at a decision as to which one of the paired objects they prefer, giving reasons for their choice. Sharing may take place with other groups or entire class.

6.17 Can You Describe It? (Intermediate)

Objective: To stimulate oral language in relation to creative thought.

Materials: A list of objects or places to describe orally, such as, an elf village, an underground thieves' hideout, a new breed of animals, a new means of transportation, or the world as seen by a turtle.

Directions: The students are to describe orally, in as much detail as possible, objects or places such as those suggested above.

Variations:
1. Students may tape their descriptions for others to hear.
2. More "real world" examples may be needed for some students.

6.18 Discussing Dilemmas (Intermediate)

Objective: To improve discussion skills through experiences of "crises."

Materials: A list of emergency situations typed on index cards, such as:

Your parents are at the store and you were supposed to take a bath before they get back in an hour. The water faucet on the bathtub broke as you were trying to turn it off, leaving water gushing everywhere. What will you do?

You are alone in the house. Suddenly you hear something moving in the garage and a crash as something has been knocked over. What will you do?

One of your very best friends has been terribly upset today at school. Tonight he calls you, crying, wanting to run away from everyone. What will you do?

Directions: The students are placed in groups of from three to eight, including a moderator. Then they are given cards with dilemmas such as the above written on them. The purpose of the round-table discussion is to share ideas on how to deal with the particular problem. The moderator keeps the discussion moving and on the topic. He or she also helps the group summarize and evaluate results. Later the ideas are shared with the class.

Variation: Brainstorming is another discussion technique that may be utilized with such situations. Remember the rules of brainstorming: no ideas may be criticized or evaluated during the brainstorming; emphasis is placed on quantity of suggestions; and group members may "piggy-back" on the ideas of others.

7 Written Composition

Writing challenges even the best student. It is no simple task to capture one's ideas, thoughts, or feelings in words that can be clearly understood by others. Written composition requires more instructional time than oral composition because there are more technical matters involved—punctuation, capitalization, sentence and paragraph sense, handwriting skills, and spelling. Written and oral composition share the same ultimate purpose, however—the organization and transmission of ideas to others.

Because of the complexity of written composition, instruction in writing skills should begin early. Very young students can begin to acquire the necessary basic skills through dictated stories. These skills are then developed through ongoing instruction in vocabulary building, cooperative writing efforts, story telling (both oral and written), analysis and imitation of stories and poems, letter and report writing, and proofreading and revision.

This chapter begins with basic writing skills activities involving a multisensory approach to writing, the development of vocabulary, and the refinement of organizational skills. These activities are followed by exercises in cooperative writing. A third set of activities focuses upon the mechanical aspects of capitalization and punctuation, and a fourth section involves practical applications of writing. The chapter then concludes with proofreading and revision activities. Exercises in creative writing—a vital and enjoyable aspect of written composition—have been incorporated into a number of this chapter's activities. Because written and oral composition share the same final purpose of communication, many of the activities in the preceding chapter on oral composition may be adapted to written composition.

BASIC WRITING SKILLS

Multisensory Activities

7.1 Draw It Out (Primary)

Objective: To enhance writing skills through visual and tactile senses.

Materials: Several yards of butcher paper, various art and writing materials.

Directions: Students are instructed to write a story on 12" strips of butcher paper. Wide butcher paper may be cut in half to provide two strips. After the story has been written with the words amply spaced, certain key words can be replaced with pictures, or can be drawn over or painted over, producing a rebus story. After the entire story has been completed it may either be put on a wall or rolled up like a scroll to be read. For incorporating *tactile* senses, the actual objects may be attached to the words.

7.2 Picture Writing (Primary)

Objective: To utilize visual senses to develop writing skills.

Materials: Writing materials, scissors, poster board, and crayons or felt-tip markers.

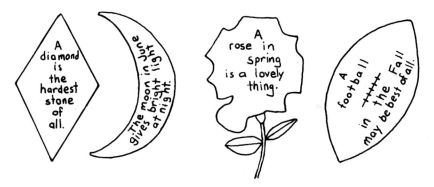

Directions: Several shapes are presented to the students. After selecting one, each student constructs that shape out of poster board. On that particular shape, the student writes about the concept or topic which the shape represents, staying within the limits of the shape itself.

7.3 Sounds and Words (Intermediate)

Objective: To incorporate auditory skills in writing.

Materials: Writing materials, records or tape recordings of various sounds and music, and examples of topics and inputs.

Topic	*Auditory Input*
The story of an aspiring ballerina	A recording of Swan Lake or music from another ballet
The story of a private eye detective on a secret mission	A tape with the detective's secret mission and the plan of execution on it
A story of a haunted house and some bizarre events on a Halloween night	A Halloween record with spooky sounds
The heartaches and joys of a zookeeper	A tape recording of zoo animals

Directions: As the student is writing (and later reading), recorded sounds are provided as background stimulus. Students are asked to compose stories on the given topic, using the music or sounds as their starting point.

Vocabulary Development

7.4 Change-a-Word Game (Intermediate)

Objectives: To increase awareness of the power of words and to spur vocabulary development.

Materials: Several sentences written on index cards (sentences should be between six and twelve words in length), a pair of dice, writing materials, a two-minute timer.

Directions: Students are placed into groups of two to four players. A sentence card is drawn from a stack and placed face up. The first player rolls a die. The number on the die indicates which word must be changed; the word may be counted from either end of the sentence. The second die is rolled; the number on this die indicates how many alternate sentences must be written, each with a replacement of the first substitute word. The student must then write as many sentences as the second die shows, with different words in the slot indicated by the first die. If correct, that student scores as many points as indicated on the second die. Play continues until a player reaches twenty-five points; or, the winner may be determined to be the player with the greatest number of points after six rounds. In case of a tie, a run-off round may be played. Here is an example of one turn.

1. Sentence: The kitten purred loudly because it missed its mother.
2. First die = 2: Change either the second word from the beginning or the second word from the end.
3. Second die = 3: After choosing to change "kitten," student produces three alternative sentences within the two-minute period: (a) The *cat* purred loudly because it missed its mother. (b) The *cougar* purred loudly because it missed its mother. (c) The *cub* purred loudly because it missed its mother.

7.5 Simile Match (Intermediate)

Objective: To facilitate student use of similes in expressive writing.

Materials: Strips of paper or cards (made from construction paper), pencil, notebook, and examples of sentences using similes.

The ocean was roaring	like a starving tiger.
The bell sounded	like an angel singing a lullaby.
The ancient book of folklore was	like the forgotten stepchild of Old Man Time.
The Indian's triumphant return was	like a shining river.

Directions: After the concept of simile has been explained, students are instructed to think of five sentences using similes and to write them on the strips of paper. The strips are divided in half before the "like" or "as" phrase markers. All of the first halves of the sentences from each of the students are gathered and placed in a box. The second halves are likewise placed in a separate box.

Students then attempt to make matches between the sentence portions. All reasonable combinations of simile pairs are written down in a notebook which can later be used as a reference.

7.6 Make and Describe (Primary or Intermediate)

Objective: To increase vocabulary through writing about an object.

Materials: Modeling clay and writing materials.

Directions: Students are given some modeling clay and told to make anything they wish to make. The student should then write a description which could include such points as color, shape, weight, texture, use.

Variations:
1. Students could later write comparisons of the physical characteristics of their objects with other objects, paying close attention to detail.
2. A self-evaluation of the student's own object could also be written in detail, including a summary of all the appealing or unappealing details about the object and an overall evaluative judgment. These could be shared if the student chose to do so.
3. Three objects could be selected by the class as the most interesting. Then each student could select the one he or she prefers, giving written reasons for the selection.
4. Oral expression (preceding or in place of written expression) may be utilized with this activity.

7.7 Describe the Place or Situation (Intermediate)

Objective: To facilitate the students' ability to write descriptive passages of places or situations.

Materials: Writing materials and a list of several unique places or situations to describe.

Places and Situations to Describe
1. An underwater cave
2. The day after a tornado
3. The starting seconds of an overtime play in a championship basketball tournament

4. A bank being robbed
5. A concert in progress
6. The last moments before a heroic rescue
7. The day of the funeral
8. A meadow glade in early winter
9. A bear caught in a trap
10. The moment the kidnapper's ransom note was received

Directions: Students are given a situation to describe in writing. Students are to write objectively from a third-person perspective. Questions such as the following need to be answered in the description as appropriate:

What is happening?
Who is involved?
What is the mood, the feeling, or the underlying emotion?
What does it look like?
What does it sound like?
What does it feel like?

Variation: The situations to be described may be personal experiences of the students and can be written from a first-person or second-person perspective.

Organizational Skills

7.8 Switch It Around (Primary or Intermediate)

Objective: To provide practice in organizational skills by rearranging sentences in various ways.

Materials: Various sentences selected from written passages, construction paper, and felt-tip markers.

Directions: On a sheet of laminated construction paper a single sentence is printed or taped. Students then take a felt-tip marker and write on the sheet as many different rearrangements of the sentence as they can think of, using only the words in the sentence.

Variations:
1. Students may be allowed to add words to their rearranged sentences as long as the meaning of the sentence is not changed.

2. Students may challenge each other to see how many different rearrangements they can create. The winner is the one who comes up with the most rearrangements that do not change the meaning of the sentence. Any sentences which change the meaning are disqualified.

7.9 Squeeze It (Primary or Intermediate)

Objective: To introduce the idea of sentence combining, that is, the combining of short sentences into longer, more complex, and more informational sentences.

Materials: Several sets of short sentences about a given subject.

Example (Primary)
It is sunny outside.
It is cold outside.

Solution
It is sunny and cold outside.

Example (Intermediate)
Bill has a dog.
The dog is brown and red.
The dog caught a rabbit.
It was after school.
Bill was walking home from school.
The day was Tuesday.

Solution
While Bill was walking home from school on Tuesday, his brown and red dog caught a rabbit.

Directions: Sentences may be composed by the teacher, the students, or taken from a written source. On index cards single simple sentences are printed. Sentences about several topics are mixed together. The student then selects the sentences that are related to each other and groups them together. After grouping these sentences together, the student tries to combine the simple sentences into longer more complex sentences.

Variation: The sentences, when combined, can form a cohesive paragraph; the student then must group the sentences correctly, combine them, and then place the sentences in correct order to form a paragraph.

7.10 Put It In Order (Intermediate)

Objective: To provide practice in putting words, sentences, or paragraphs in correct sequential order.

Materials: Sets of sentences, paragraphs, and stories.

Directions: Type or print the sentences into single lines, so as to avoid any configuration clues. (Sentences may be taken from a story or a reading book or may be originally written; they should represent various types of expository and narrative texts—recipes, fiction paragraphs, newspaper articles, and the like.) Paragraphs may remain intact. Cut the sentences into words; cut the paragraphs into single line sentences; or cut the stories into paragraphs. Mix up the pieces and place them in envelopes. Direct the students to put the words, sentences, or paragraphs in correct sequence.

Variations:
1. For a simpler task use shorter sentences, paragraphs, or stories; for a more difficult task use longer and more complex sentences, paragraphs, and stories.
2. For primary students comic strips can be cut up by frames, shuffled, and then placed in sequence.

COOPERATIVE AND STRUCTURED WRITING

7.11 Story Pieces (Primary)

Objective: To provide students the opportunity to write a story in conjunction with others: group composition.

Materials: Writing materials, timer, and several story starters.

Bill and John were digging for clams. All at once Bill's shovel hit something that made a hollow sound.

Directions: Read aloud a story starter to a group of four or five students seated in a circle. One student begins writing a short story using the story starter. At the end of three minutes the student is stopped and told to pass the paper to the left. That student then reads what has been written and continues the story. After five to eight more minutes that student is told to pass the paper to the left. This process continues until the paper has gone around the circle. The student who originally started the story then reads what has been written and writes the end to the story. The story should then be read aloud or typed for all to enjoy.

Variation: For some really bizarre stories, have student fold under the paper on which they have been writing before passing the paper. The students then continue writing their own original stories, each time folding the paper under again. At the end of the round, the page is unfolded and the stories are read.

7.12 Bridge the Gap (Primary or Intermediate)

Objective: To increase students' awareness of structure in writing.

Materials: Construction paper and various passages taken from reading books, children's trade books, or other story or informational material.

She really didn't know what to do.

- -

- -

Her friend hadn't come back, and she was tired of holding on.

Directions: Select a story passage and choose two sentences from that story. These two sentences are printed onto a sheet of colored construction paper. The students are given copies of the page and told to write something that could connect the sentences into a logical paragraph. (These need not be similar to the original passage of the text.) For a less complicated task, single sentences with missing words may be used, with the student supplying the missing words.

7.13 Use the Pattern (Primary or Intermediate)

Objective: To provide experience with patterned writing.

Materials: Appropriate books of stories and poems and a bulletin board display.

```
What is Round?

"A Kiss            "Round is
 is Round"          a Pancake"

What else is round?
```

Directions: Reproduce patterned poems on the bulletin board. Provide for close study of the model, discuss the model, encourage questions about patterns in the model and other features. Efforts may begin with whole class contributions, move to small groups, and finally to individuals. First drafts may be refined and the patterned story or poem illustrated—and an illustrated typed copy may be made into a book.

Here are a few collections of stories and poems that teachers have found useful when teaching patterned writing.

Aiken, Conrad. *Cats and Bats and Things with Wings*. New York: Athenuem, 1965.

Brandenburg, Franz. *I Once Knew a Man*. New York: Macmillan Company, 1970.

Cameron, Polly. *"I Can't" Said the Ant*. New York: Scholastic Books, 1969.

Charlip, Remy. *What Good Luck! What Bad Luck!* New York: Scholastic Books, 1970.

DeRegneirs, Beatrice Schenk. *May I Bring a Friend*? New York: Athenuem, 1964.

Donomaka, Janina. *If All the Seas Were One Sea*. New York: Macmillan, 1971.

Gregory, Horace, and Mary Zaturenska, comps. *The Silver Swan: Poem of Mystery and Romance*. New York: Holt, Rinehart and Winston, 1968.

Holdsworth, William Curtis. *The Gingerbread Boy*. New York: Farrar, Strauss, and Giroux, 1970.

Jacobs, Leland B. *Poetry for Chuckles and Grins*. Champaign, IL: Garrard, 1968.

Kraus, Robert. *Whose Mouse Are You?* New York: Macmillan, 1970.

Kredensen, Gail, and Stanley Mack. *One Dancing Drum*. New York: S.G. Phillips, 1971.

Langstaff, John. *Soldier, Soldier, Won't You Marry Me?* New York: Doubleday, 1972.

Martin, Jr., Bill. *David Was Mad*. New York: Holt, Rinehart and Winston, 1971.

O'Neill, Mary. *Hailstones and Halibut Bones*. New York: Scholastic Books, 1961.

Oppenheim, Joan. *Have You Seen Trees?* New York: Young Scott, 1967.

Sullivan, Joan. *Round Is a Pancake*. New York: Holt, Rinehart and Winston, 1967.

CAPITALIZATION AND PUNCTUATION

7.14 Capital Letter Pop Up (Primary)

Objective: To provide experience in recognizing proper nouns which must be capitalized.

Materials: Sets of sentences (which contain proper nouns) of eight words.

Directions: Eight students are seated in a circle. Read aloud a sentence and point at one student for each word of the sentence, going around the circle *counterclockwise*. The student who was pointed toward with a proper noun must stand (pop-up) as soon as the word is spoken.

7.15 Punctuation Hold Up (Primary)

Objective: To provide practice in applying correct punctuation marks.

Materials: Cards with a period, a comma, an exclamation mark, and a question mark drawn on them. List of sentences which use the four marks of punctuation.

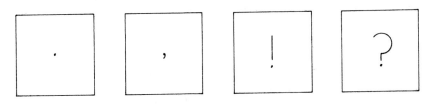

Directions: Students are divided into two teams. A sentence is read by the teacher or leader. The team member who is "up" must hold up the appropriate punctuation mark. A point is scored each time a team member holds up the correct card. The opposing team can gain points by correcting mistakes of the opposing team. Teams alternate turns. Play ends when everyone has had a turn (or two turns).

7.16 Capitalization and Punctuation Monopoly (Intermediate)

Objective: To improve basic capitalization and punctuation skills.

Materials: A piece of cardboard, poster board or an old Monopoly board for the game board, play money or Monopoly money, dice, Monopoly tokens, and index cards to use for questions cards and deeds.

Capitalization Questions
1. Which word is *always* capitalized in a sentence?
2. Which word in the salutation of a letter is capitalized?
3. Which word in a closing is *not* capitalized?
4. On a calendar, what two items should always be capitalized?
5. What is the name of an organization that should be capitalized?

Punctuation Questions
1. What punctuation is used after initials?
2. When is a question mark used?
3. What punctuation is used before and after appositives?
4. What does the apostrophe indicate in "Bill's ball"?
5. What punctuation is used at the end of a line to show a divided word?

Contrac-tion Avenue	Question Mark Drive	Period Lane	Exclama-tion Mark Drive	Capital Railroad	Capital Letter Corner	Free Parking
Capital Letter Corner						Semi-colon Gas Co.
Semi-colon Street		Capitalization Question Cards				Punctua-tion Ins. Collector Pay $100.
Apostro-phe Avenue						Go Back 3 Spaces
Comma Blvd.		Punctuation Question Cards				Capital Electric Company
Punctua-tion Place						Period Airlines
GO Collect $200.00	Quota-tion Mark Park	Capital Water Works	Go to JAIL	Comma Bus Lines	Roll Again	JAIL

Directions:

1. Shuffle the question cards and put them in the appropriate place.
2. Have each player roll the dice. The highest number goes first and around the board to that player's left.
3. The first player rolls the dice and moves his or her token. If the player lands on a street or place with a punctuation term on it, player will draw a card from the punctuation questions. If he or she lands on capitalization, a capitalization question will be drawn.

    If the player answers the question correctly, he or she will receive ten dollars from the bank and the opportunity to buy the property.

    If the question is answered incorrectly, the player has to pay the bank ten dollars and cannot buy the street. If the street is owned by another player, the player must pay rent if the answer to the question is incorrect, but if correct, will not have to pay rent.
4. The rest of the rules are like the regular Monopoly game.

7.17 Cartoon Quotes (Intermediate)

Objective: To provide students with experience in transcribing dialogue to written conversation, using quotation marks accurately.

Materials: Comic strip cartoons and comic book cartoons.

Directions: Students are given a comic strip to transcribe. The words spoken by the characters are to be placed in quotation marks with appropriate punctuation marks. Finally, the students add explanatory phrases such as, "John exclaimed," "Then Sally said," and descriptions to fill in the story.

Variation: A conversation can also be transcribed using a tape recording of a discussion.

PRACTICAL APPLICATIONS

7.18 Purposeful Letters (Intermediate)

Objective: To provide practice in writing letters for a variety of purposes.

Materials: Writing materials and three small boxes.

Box 1 Letter Types	Box 2 Topics	Box 3 Letter Parts
a. Complaints	a. Flowers are being picked by school children.	a. Opening Paragraph
b. Compliments	b. Your dog is a prize winner.	b. Reason or Idea 1
c. Suggestion	c. Why not purple cabbages?	c. Reason or Idea 2
d. Friendly	d. The trip to the Island of Hulu Gulu was . . .	d. Reason or Idea 3
e. Business	e. The shoes have not been received.	e. Closing Paragraph
f. Expressing opinions	f. Our class should have a Book Fair.	f. Opening Paragraph

Directions: One box is labeled Letter Types. A second box is labeled Topics to Discuss. A third box is labeled Letter Parts. Strips of paper are cut and categories of ideas are written on them and placed in appropriate boxes. Students select one strip of paper from each box. The writing task is to write the paragraph identified on the strip from Box 3 about the topic from Box 2 in the style of the slip chosen from Box 1.

Variation: For more advanced letter writing, omit the use of Box 3, and have the students write the entire letter.

7.19 Creating Form Letters (Intermediate)

Objective: To provide the student with a general format for various types of letter writing.

Materials: Writing materials, a pair of dice, and a notebook.

Directions: The student rolls the dice. The number that is rolled corresponds to one of the following *types* of letters.

Number Rolled	Type of Letter
2	Complaint Letter
3 or 4	Compliment Letter
5	Editorial Letter
6	Friendly Letter
7	Business Letter
8, 9, 10	Thank You Letter
11	Birthday/Get Well Letter
12	Sympathy Letter

The student again rolls the dice for a number which corresponds with one of the following *parts* of a letter:

Number Rolled	Parts of Letter
2	Return Address
3	Inside Address and Greeting
4	Opening Paragraph
5	Reason or Idea 1
6	Reason or Idea 2
7	Reason or Idea 3
8	Closing Paragraph
9 or 10	Envelope Format
11 or 12	Closing and Signature

Students are paired. The students, at each turn, write the part of the letter identified by the second roll of the dice, in the type of letter identified by the first roll of the dice.

(numbers rolled=8 and 5)

Return Address

Inside Address

Greeting

Opening paragraph

Reason 1

One reason that I like the sweater so much is that it is my favorite color.

Reason 2

Reason 3

Closing Paragraph

Closing

Signature

Variations:

1. Over a period of time the activity may be extended so that all the letters have been completed.
2. If the rolling of the dice takes too long toward the end of the activity, only one die may be rolled, with a condensing of the lists.

7.20 Social Note Center (Intermediate)

Objective: To provide familiarity with social note writing.

Materials: Filmstrips and projector, model social notes on transparencies, tape recorder and tapes, and *The First Book of Letter Writing* by Helen Jacobson and Florence Mischell (New York: Watts, 1957).

Assignment Sheet: Writing Social Notes

1. View the filmstrips about
   a. thank-you notes
   b. invitations
   c. cheer-up notes
   d. congratulation notes
2. Study the model social notes on the transparencies.
3. Turn on the tape recorder and listen as the tape points out important things to include in social notes.
4. Read about social notes in *The First Book of Letter Writing.*
5. Make a list of suggestions you have learned about writing social notes. Compare your list with your partner.
6. If you feel you can write a social note, write one.
7. Let your partner proofread your note.
8. Put your revised note in your folder for the teacher to check.

Directions: Organize materials so that the learner is directed toward the writing of social notes, such as filmstrips on the topic; a model social note on transparencies; a tape pointing out important items to include in social notes; a trade book dealing with letter writing. Students are asked to do the eight items listed on the assignment sheet. This is usually a part of a learning center established in one part of the classroom.

7.21 The Six Detectives (Primary or Intermediate)

Objective: To facilitate report writing by providing some organizational structure for incorporating information.

Materials: Writing materials, resources for research (encyclopedias, dictionaries, newspapers, and history books), a list of interesting topics for report (the Loch Ness Monster, recent events, sports), and paper hats or other detective disguise outfits.

Directions: Groups of six students are assigned a topic for research. Each student is given a paper detective hat. Each student then puts on the hat and begins to research all of the information pertaining to the "who," "when," "where," "what," "why," or "how" of a topic. After the materials have been gathered, each detective is responsible for writing one or more paragraphs reporting his or her research. The students then put their paragraphs together to form a joint report which may be given orally to the class. Following the oral report of the group, each student writes up a "detective report" which contains all the information of that particular section. Each student also writes an "Introduction to the Case" and a "Case Conclusion"; the group decides on the best ones or incorporates several to come up with an introduction and an ending to the report. The entire report, consisting of the "Introduction to the Case," six detective reports, and the "Case Conclusion," is placed into a folder for others to read.

Variations:

1. This activity may also be done by each individual student. The student simply changes hats every day some new topic is to be researched. The following order is suggested:

Day	Detective	Topic
1	Chief	Introduction to the Case
2	Agent What	"What" is the Case?

3	Agent	When	"When" did everything take place?
4	Detective	Who	"Who" was involved?
5	Detective	Where	"Where" did it all take place?
6	Private Eye	How	"How" did it happen?
7	Private Eye	Why	"Why" did it happen?
8	Chief		Case Conclusion

At the conclusion of the project all of the reports are assembled into a case (in a notebook or file), which can then be filed in the "Detective Cases" cabinet.

2. Students can also create their own mysteries or cases which they then write up.

7.22 Point of View (Intermediate)

Objective: To provide practice in informational report writing in one of the content areas.

Materials: List of topics and characters.

Report Topic		The Character
Historical	The inventions of Benjamin Franklin	The first pair of eyeglasses invented
	Roman gladiator	A dungeon cell deep within the walls of the arena
Authentic	Jacques Cousteau's underworld	An air tank
Musical	The life of Bach	The nineteenth child of Bach
	The symphony orchestra	A cello
Art	The paintings of Leonardo da Vinci	Da Vinci's painting pallette
Physical Education	The skills of field hockey	The field hockey referee's whistle

Directions: Have the students research a topic of interest and then write their information in note form. Then have the students write the report using all the information obtained and assuming a character's viewpoint.

7.23 Be a Newspaper Writer (Intermediate)

Objectives: To provide practice in writing items as found in newspapers.

Materials: Newspapers and a set of ideas as suggested.

Assignment Sheet: Newspaper Reporter

1. Write a *classified ad*: Write an ad to sell something you own and want to sell, like an old basketball.
2. Write a *front page story*: Write a headline and a story about it.
3. Write a *comic strip*: Write a cartoon strip about imaginary people and events.
4. Write an *editorial*: Write your point-of-view about a topic.
5. Write a *"home" article*: Write a recipe or give some safety tips.
6. Write an *advice column*: Write a column with letters and answers.
7. Write a *weather report*: Write a paragraph giving weather forecast.
8. Write a *joke or riddle*: Write a joke or riddle for newspaper "filler."

Directions: After studying the various parts of the newspaper, students should read the set of ideas as proposed above and write one of the activities. The results can be compared and shared.

Variations: Other "newspaper" possibilities include a letter to the editor, a poem, a movie or television review, and a crossword puzzle.

PROOFREADING AND REVISION

7.24 Check Your Composition (Intermediate)

Objective: To provide practice in rewriting compositions.

Materials: Cooperatively developed standards charts.

Check Your Composition

1. Are the main ideas clear?
2. Are details specific?
3. Is it in logical order?
4. Are sentences varied and well developed?
5. Is vocabulary varied?

---

1. No sentence fragments
2. No punctuation errors
3. No word usage errors
4. No capitalization errors
5. No misspelled words

Directions: Have students cooperatively develop a chart such as illustrated. Encourage students to check a recent composition, using their standards.

7.25 Revise Your Composition (Intermediate)

Objective: To provide practice in revision of written product.

Materials: Written products and a cooperatively—developed scale.

Revise Your Composition

1. What did you try to do to improve this paper?
2. What is a good point of your paper? Circle a sentence or two that you feel are well done.
3. What are some points that you think you need more help?
4. What is the area you feel is best in this paper?
   a. content
   b. organization
   c. mechanics
5. What should you do next to improve your written expression?

Directions: Have students cooperatively develop a chart such as cited above. Encourage students to use it in revising a recent written product.

7.26 Marks for Improvement (Intermediate)

Objective: To help students interpret proofreading marks.

Materials: Passage, as below, with proofreading marks.

My Vacation Plans

On Sunday my dad, mother, and I will leave on our vacation. We will stay at a hotel on the beech. When we get there I'm going to go swimming. Then I will go back into the Hotel room and watch TV until bedtime. On Monday we will, breakfast. Then go swimming. I'll stay on the beach until lunch time. [In the afternoon I will play, in the park. I will visit some interesting places.] Then I'll read until bedtime. That's what I will do every day. We will come home on Thursday. We went to this same place last year and I enjoyed it very much. I hope I have as much fun as I did last year.

Directions: Review the proofreading marks and their meaning.

¶ paragraph needed
sp spelling error
frag. fragment (incomplete sentence)
ᵛ apostrophe needed
∕ small letter needed
∧ insert missing word
∕ delete
∧ comma needed
⊙ period needed
[ ] combine into one sentence

Then distribute a copy of the story to the class. Students may work in pairs, interpreting the proofreading marks and rewriting the story as suggested.

Variation: Paragraphs may be edited for single items, such as punctuation or capitalization.

8 Spelling

The spelling activities in this chapter involve a variety of topics: phoneme-grapheme relationships; structural analysis skills; spelling patterns; special categories of words; study procedures; proof reading; and dictionary use.

Associating printed symbols (*graphemes*) with the speech sounds they represent (*phonemes*) is a basic part of spelling. In English this sound-symbol association is somewhat irregular. There is sufficient regularity, however, for students to be taught phonic generalizations which will enable them to spell a large percentage of words that they will encounter in school. Nonetheless, because many words are not spelled as they sound, spelling study should not be limited to the phonic elements.

There are some common spelling patterns often recommended for elementary school study.

Pattern	Example	Exception
C-V-C (short vowel)	cat	put
C-V-C+e (long vowel, silent *e*)	save	have
C-V-V-C (long first vowel)	coat	break
C-V-r (controlled, preceding vowel)	far	burn
C-V (long vowel)	go	do

Exceptions (and many are very common words) are noted above to caution the reader. After the generalization is operational for most of the students, the exceptions, their frequency, and significance can be discussed. No pattern should be taught as consistent.

Structural analysis skills are those involving identification of prefixes, suffixes, and root words; inflectional endings; contractions; compound words; and syllabication and accent. When words are spelled through units, more than single graphemes or letters are considered. Prefixes and suffixes are *morphemes* (the smallest units of meaning) added to root words to form new words called *derivatives*. The result is a change in meaning and may be accompanied by a change in the part of speech of the root word. Prefixes are placed before root words, and suffixes are placed after root words (*un* in *unrelated*; *ful* in *joyful*). *Inflectional endings* are morphemes which when added to nouns change the number (*s* in *girls*), case (*'s* of *girl's*), or gender (*ess* in *hostess*); when added to verbs inflectional endings change the tense (*ed* in *walked*) or person (*s* in *walks*); and when they are added to adjectives they change the degree (*est* in *meanest*); they also may change the part of speech of a word (*ly* in *slowly*). The new words that are produced by adding inflectional endings are called *variants*. *Contractions* are combinations of two words with one or more letters left out; the missing letters are indicated by an apostrophe (*can't* for *cannot*). *Compound words* are composed of two words which when combined form a new word (*cowboy*). Since many phonic generalizations apply not only to single syllable words but to syllables within multisyllabic words as well, *syllabication* and *accent* are important structural analysis skills.

Study of certain *categories* of words (homonyms, homographs, synonyms, antonyms, acronyms, multiple-meaning words, and abbreviations) should also be helpful to the pupil in learning to spell. *Homonyms* are words that sound alike but have different meanings and spellings (*blue, blew*). *Homographs* are words that are spelled alike but have different pronunications and meanings (*bow*: a type of tie; *bow*: to bend at the waist). *Synonyms* are words that have approximately the same meanings (*beautiful, pretty*). *Antonyms* are words with nearly opposite meanings (*hot, cold*). *Acronyms* are words composed of the first letters or syllables of the different words in multiple-word terms (*radar—radio detecting and ranging*). An example of a *multiple-meaning word* is *run*; *Co.* is the *abbreviation* for Company.

Ernest Horn suggested the teaching of only those spelling rules that apply, with but few exceptions, to a large number of words. For example:

1. Words ending in silent *e* usually drop the final *e* before the addition of suffixes beginning with a vowel, but they keep the *e* before the addition of suffixes beginning with a consonant. Illustration: make—making; time—timely.
2. When a word ends in a consonant and *y*, change the *y* to *i* before adding all suffixes except those beginning with *i*. Do not change *y* to *i* in adding suffixes to words ending in a vowel and *y* or when adding a suffix beginning with *i*. Illustration: baby, babies, babying, play, played, playing.
3. Words of one syllable or words accented on the last syllable, ending in a single consonant preceded by a single vowel, double

the final consonant when adding a suffix beginning with a vowel. Illustration: run—running; begin—beginning.
4. The letter *q* is always followed by *u* in common English words. Illustration: quick, queen, quiet.
5. English words do not end in *v*.
6. Proper nouns and most adjectives formed from proper nouns should begin with capital letters.[1]

The teacher must give careful attention to the pupils' methods of study and their use of the study period. The study period should be a learning period. Only those students who made errors in the pretest should be required to study spelling words; but the others need not be excused from subsequent tests. Effective study requires that each student work only on his or her own difficulties; therefore locating the difficulties must be the first step. The following lists steps for studying spelling.

1. Pronounce the word clearly to yourself.
2. Carefully copy the word, noting how the sounds in the word are represented by the letters.
3. Look at your copy and say the letters twice.
4. Cover the word or close your eyes. Pretend you are writing the word on paper twice.
5. Write the word on paper without looking at your book or the copy you made.
6. Check your word. Did you spell it correctly?
7. If you missed the word, go over all the steps again. When you are sure you can spell the word, study the next word.

As elementary school teachers know, carelessness, indifference, and failure to proofread are major causes of errors in written work. *Proofreading* exercises are designed to develop in students a firm habit of attention to detail. Proofreading should begin early; by the third grade, a more formal approach to proofreading can be presented. Proofreading is a visual task which focuses upon the spelling errors of the writer. Misspelling words that appear on basic spelling lists must be rigorously overcome. Time must be provided for proofreading, correction, and recopying. The activities must be an integral part of instruction—perceived as

[1]Ernest A. Horn, "Spelling," *Encyclopedia of Educational Research*, 3d ed. (American Educational Association, 1960), p. 1345. Reprinted by permission of the Macmillan Company.

important by teachers and students. An individual teacher focusing on this skill may produce some improvement. To be most effective, however, a total, school-wide program of proofreading should be adopted.

Dictionaries can help students determine correct spellings. Before using a dictionary, students must be able to locate a designated word with reasonable facility. Three important skills are necessary for effective dictionary use: knowledge of alphabetical order; ability to use guide words; and ability to locate variants and derivatives in the dictionary by locating root words.

Whereas this chapter consists of activities which can be used to teach and reinforce spelling skills, several other spelling-related activities are presented in this volume: word-concept activities (10.2) and word-recreational activities (11.8, 11.9, 11.10, 11.12, 11.13, 11.15).

PHONEME-GRAPHEME CORRESPONDENCES

Phoneme Change, Meaning Change

8.1 Spelling Ladders (Primary)

Objective: To help students notice the difference made in a word by changing one letter at a time.

Materials: Sets of spelling ladders.

Directions: Instruct students to draw word ladders as shown. Starting at the lowest rung of the ladder, the players change one letter at a time (making a new word) until reaching the highest rung. (Answers for the three ladders shown may be, A: bag, ban, bat, cat, cot, got, hot, hut, nut, put; B: can, fan, fat, hat, hit, lit, pit, pot, rot, tot; C: bad, dad, fad, fed, led, lad, mad, pad, sad, had; other words are possible.)

Variation: *Antonyms* may be used for the bottom and top rungs, with the same objective: *dry,* day, may, mat, met, *wet.* Some antonyms that may be used include: *love, hate; man, boy; cat, dog; seek, find.*

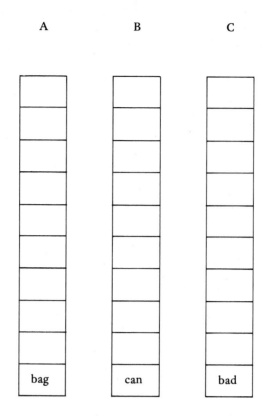

Grapheme Sequence

8.2 Word Scramble (Primary)

Objective: To help students attend to the sequencing of letters that spell a word.

Materials: A series of word scrambles as illustrated below.

1. | o   b |
    |---|
    | x |

2. | h   a |
    |---|
    | e   c |

3. | u   d |
    |---|
    | k   c |

4. | a   f |
    |---|
    | l   h |

5. | o   t |
    |---|
    | o   f |

6. | k c l |
    |---|
    | c o |

7. | n   r |
    |---|
    | i   a |

8. | e s o |
    |---|
    | h s |

9. | s r a |
    |---|
    | g s |

Directions: Ask the students to unscramble the letters to form a word. Answers to the above are: 1. box; 2. each; 3. duck; 4. half; 5. foot; 6. clock; 7. rain; 8. shoes; and 9. grass.

Variation: This activity could easily be adjusted to intermediate level by using more difficult words.

8.3 Word Search (Intermediate)

Objective: To give practice in recognizing correct sequence of letters to form a word.

Materials: Duplicating master; typewriter and/or pen; and a puzzle similar to the one below.

Spelling Word Search Puzzle

Q	E	N	I	Z	A	G	A	M
N	L	A	N	R	B	R	O	O
R	A	T	S	E	L	D	M	T
A	O	U	I	T	E	S	T	T
E	C	R	D	L	W	K	I	O
H	R	E	E	H	C	Y	F	B

Starter words

able	earn	model
arm	east	nature
blew	fit	rats
bottom	inside	sky
cheer	keen	star
coal	magazine	such

Directions: Distribute copies of the puzzle. Instruct students to locate the words listed below the puzzle and circle the words. Tell them that the words may go horizontal, vertical, or diagonal, and either forward or backward.

Grapheme Groups

8.4 The -*ay* Word Family (Intermediate)

Objective: To develop structural analysis skills involving grapheme families, here the -*ay* word group.

Materials: Worksheet with a list of definitions, with the directions for writing the word for each definition: one letter or more than one letter can be added in front of -*ay*.

1. What you want to go outside and do _____
2. What a potter works with _____
3. What the knight would do to the dragon _____
4. What you do when you put something off _____
5. A kind of team race run in track _____

Directions: A small group (four to six) is given definitions of words that contain -*ay* spelling. Students try to supply as many words as possible independently; comparison and discussion of answers then may be encouraged. (For the above example, the words are: play, clay, slay, delay, and relay.)

Variations:
1. Many grapheme groups can be used in such an activity: the -*at* family; the -*oy* family; the -*owl* family; the -*ap* family; the -*ing* family; the -*up* family, and others.
2. Students could also make up clues for their own word family games.
3. Primary students can form words by adding a single letter to each of these common endings: -*all*; -*and*; -*old*; -*an*; -*in*; -*ike*; -*ate*; -*ill*.

8.5 Wagon Affixes (Intermediate)

Objective: To develop structural analysis skills in constructing words by the addition of common prefixes and suffixes.

Materials: Poster board, pen, and scissors.

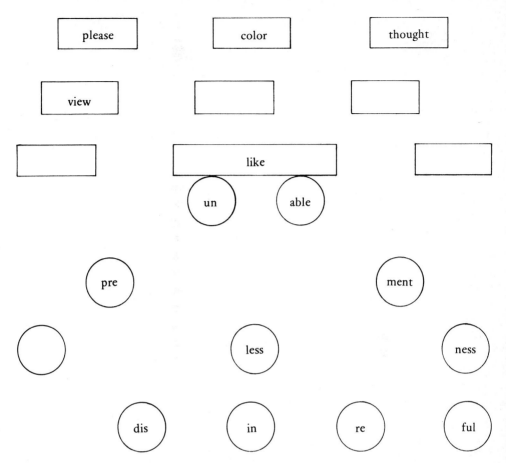

Directions: Draw the outline of a wagon on a sheet of poster board. Cut out several wagon body forms and wheel forms. Write root words on the wagon body cutouts and write prefixes and suffixes on the wheel cutouts. Leave one wheel cutout blank. Let two students or two teams take turns in making words with affixes by using the wheel and wagon body cutouts. Each student or team gets one point for a word made with a root word and either a prefix or a suffix, or two points for a word made with a root and both a prefix and suffix. If a student makes a nonword, a point is lost. A student may serve as monitor.

8.6 Write an Ending (Primary)

Objective: To develop structural analysis skills by constructing words with common inflectional endings.

Materials: A listing of inflectional endings and index cards with root words written on them.

Inflectional Endings   *Root Words*

1. -s
2. -es
3. -ed
4. -ing
5. -er
6. -est
7. -ly
8. -ess

cool	host
warm	keep
play	girl
jump	truck

Directions: Give each player a stack of root word cards. Let the students take turns. The first player tries to write a word combining the first inflectional ending with one of the root word cards. If successful, a point is awarded; if not, a point is lost. Used root word cards are out of play for the remainder of the game. The second player tries to write a word by combining the second inflectional ending with one of the root word cards. Each inflectional ending is taken in turn by the player. The game ends when one player runs out of cards.

8.7 Compound Lace-Up (Intermediate)

Objective: To develop structural analysis skills in constructing compound words.

Materials: Poster board, yarn or string cut in various lengths, paper fasteners, and felt-tip markers.

Directions: On one side of the poster, list words that can be joined to other words to form compound words. On the other side make a similar list, giving only the first letter of the word. Punch holes beside the entries on each side. Place paper fasteners in the holes. Attach one end of yarn or string to the fasteners beside the list on the left-side of the poster board.

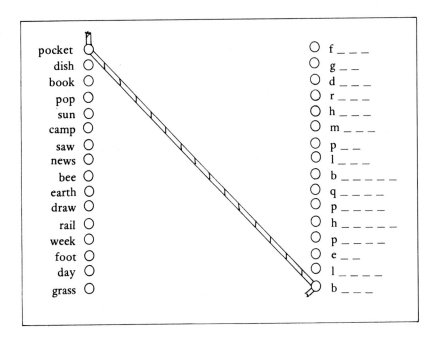

The student attaches the free end of the yarn or string to the fastener beside the letter that suggests a compound word. On a separate piece of paper, the child writes the compound word. An answer card showing the correct lacing (that is, the correct spelling of the compound words) can be made available to the students.

8.8 Contraction Puzzle (Primary)

Objective: To develop structural analysis skills in spelling contractions.

Materials: Contraction puzzle envelopes.

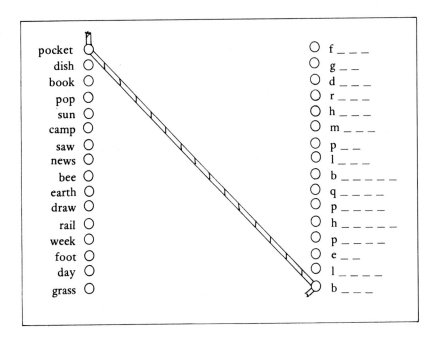

Directions: Four or six puzzle pieces are placed in one envelope. The puzzle pieces are covered with clear contact paper to permit writing on the blank side (and then cleaning off). The player writes the contractions for the words in the envelope. To check, on the back of the card is the correct answer.

Variations:
1. A similar activity can be developed to reverse the game. The students are to spell the words from which various contractions are formed.
2. A similar activity can involve apostrophes in possessives.

Multigraphemic Phonemes

8.9 Find the Rhyme (Primary)

Objective: To facilitate students' ability to recognize a phoneme represented by several graphemes.

Materials: A rhyming word puzzle.

The *um* Rhyming Word Puzzle
(number of rhyming words: 7)

d	t	i	g	o
u	p	l	u	m
m	n	e	m	a
b	u	m	u	d
e	s	o	m	e
c	o	m	e	x

Directions: Ask each student to think of words with the same ending sound, such as *um*. On the chalkboard, list the words that the students discover and then quickly prepare and distribute a word puzzle as shown. (Words for primary students should only be placed horizontally or vertically.) Each student tries to find the rhyming words. Rhyming words are circled as they are found.

Variations:
1. Students may enjoy listing rhyming words, making their own word puzzle, and exchanging them with a partner to find the rhyming words.
2. Older students may circle words on the graph in all directions, including backwards and diagonally.

8.10 The /f/ Game (Primary or Intermediate)

Objective: To provide practice in associating a common phoneme represented by a variety of graphemes.

Materials: A list of words containing /f/, such as *fish, phone, laugh, graph, calf, rough, shuffle, cafe, raffle, gruff.* A sheet of paper squared as shown.

f	ph
ff	gh

Directions: Divide students into teams. A team leader calls out the words containing the /f/ phoneme. The team players write them in the appropriate squares.

Variations:
1. Individual words may be written on cards, shuffled, and sorted according to the grapheme representing the phoneme.
2. Pupils may think of words that apply to the phoneme-grapheme correspondence.
3. Other phonemes, such as /c/ with the /s/ or /k/ sound, and appropriate words may be used in this game.

SPELLING PATTERNS

Regular Spelling Patterns

8.11 What's the Pattern? (Intermediate)

Objective: To provide practice with the spelling pattern C-V-C+*e* (long vowel, silent *e*).

Materials: A set of cards, with the front illustrated by phonetic spelling. On the other side the traditional graphemic representation of the word should appear.

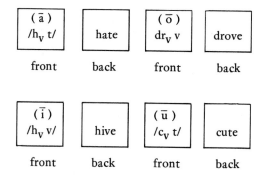

| ($\bar{a}$) /h_v t/ | hate | ($\bar{o}$) dr_v v | drove |

front   back   front   back

| ($\bar{i}$) /h_v v/ | hive | ($\bar{u}$) /c_v t/ | cute |

front   back   front   back

Directions: Stack the cards in a pile with the front side visible. The first player deciphers the phonic representation, then checks the spelling on the back of the card. The card is then placed at the bottom of the stack. Correctly spelled words score one point. The player to the left then has the next turn. After an agreed upon number of rounds of play, the player with the most points wins the game.

Some long *a* vowel words that might be used include: *rate, fate, pane, save.* Some long *i* vowel words that may be used include: *dime, ripe, hide, bite, stripe, quite, site, wine, fine, ride, snipe.* Some long *u* vowel words that might be used include: *cute, use, fuse, mule.* Some long *o* vowel words that might be used include: *hope, rode, note, dote, code.*

Variations:

1. The exceptions to this pattern (*love, have, give, come*) should be discussed.
2. A similar activity can be utilized for the other common spelling patterns. See the introduction to this chapter for a list of regular patterns.

8.12 Adding -s or -es (Primary)

Objective: To help students form plurals, distinguishing between words that add -s and those that add -es.

Materials: A soft rubber ball or a beanbag. Twenty nouns written in singular form on the chalkboard and numbered.

1.	box	11.	bush
2.	store	12.	lunch
3.	boy	13.	room
4.	thing	14.	apple
5.	beach	15.	branch
6.	dress	16.	dish
7.	gas	17.	letter
8.	class	18.	bird
9.	doll	19.	toy
10.	fox	20.	wagon

Directions: Each group has five members—four players and a leader. The leader for a group is given a list of twenty nouns and their plurals. The leader calls the number of one of the nouns and throws the ball or beanbag to a player in the group. That player goes to the chalkboard and writes the plural form of the noun. When a player correctly forms the plural, the leader calls "Hit." The player who correctly formed the plural gets to call out a number and throw the ball or beanbag to another player in the group. The procedure is repeated until the twenty nouns have been made plural.

If a player misspells a plural, the leader calls "Miss" and erases the word. A player gets one point for each correct plural. The highest score wins.

Variation: For many activities to practice spelling rules, see P. Anderson and P. Groff, *Resource Materials for Teachers of Spelling* (Minneapolis, MN: Burgess, 1968).

Syllabic Spelling Pattern

8.13 Spell by Syllable (Intermediate)

Objective: To provide practice in spelling in syllables.

Materials: Game board on a piece of poster board; felt-tip markers; spinner with numbers for 1 to 4; tokens for players (buttons or other similar materials); cards with words of different number of syllables written on them and stacked according to number of syllables—one syllable words in one pile, two syllable words in a second, and so on. A sample race route on the poster board.

Start Here	1	3	2	4	2	1	3
							4
4	2	1	4	3	1	2	
2							
	2	1	4	3	4	2	1
							3
End	3	2	1	2	4	3	

Directions: Players place their game tokens on the "Start Here" space. One person acts as a monitor and does not play. Each player, in turn, spins the spinner. A "1" indicates that the token must be moved to the nearest "1" on the board. The monitor then draws a card from the stack of one syllable words. If the player spells it correctly, the token remains on the number to which the player moved. If the player is incorrect, the token is returned to the start. On each turn the player must move to the next appropriate number that is ahead of his or her position on the board. The first player to reach the end wins. Here are some sample words for the monitor to use (Grade 4 words):

One syllable	Two syllables	Three syllables	Four syllables
bank	address	beginning	arithmetic
bay	almost	carnival	automobile
bees	angry	conductor	interested
bike	arrow	December	remembering
blow	August	decided	watermelon
blue	balloon	different	wonderfully
boots	basement	elephant	explanation
clay	belong	finally	relationship
club	beside	following	togetherness
cook	baker	furniture	

Variations:

1. The words may be placed on the race course and the players divide the words into syllables as they land on them, using the spinner to determine the moves on the game board.
2. The list of words may be chosen from one particular area, such as mathematics terms: *square, equals, pyramid, arithmetic.*

SPECIAL CATEGORY OF WORDS

8.14 Homophone Matching Game (Intermediate)

Objective: To provide practice with matching homophones.

Materials: Deck of homophone cards.

pane	pain

Cards can be prepared for such homophones as:

an, Ann, Anne	hair, hare	rain, reign, rein
ate, eight	hear, here	read, red
bass, base	hole, whole	right, write, wright, rite
be, bee	in, inn	road, rode, rowed
bear, bare	led, lead	sail, sale
brake, break	lie, lye	sea, see
cent, scent	made, maid	sight, site, cite
close, clothes	main, mane, Maine	son, sun
course, coarse	missed, mist	stare, stair
dear, deer	no, know	tale, tail
fair, fare	one, won	threw, through
feet, feat	paced, paste	very, vary
flower, flour	pail, pale	wait, weight
gate, gait	pare, pair, pear	way, weigh
groan, grown	peace, piece	wood, would
guessed, guest	plane, plain	your, you're

Directions: This activity should have no more than four players in a group, although several groups may play simultaneously. After discussing homophones with the students, prepare a deck of homophone cards, with one card for each homophone in a set. Spread the cards out, face down. The first player picks up a card and reads the word and then spells the *matching* homophone. If correct, the card is laid aside as one point. If incorrectly spelled, the card is returned face down, and the turn passes to the next player. Ideally, discussion should follow the activity and should focus on the difference in *meaning* of the matched homophones.

Variations:

1. Directions can be altered so that the first player picks up a card and reads the word. He or she then takes another card to try to find a matching homophone. If nonmatching cards are turned up, the cards are returned face down, and the turn passes to the next player. As long as a player can continue to match cards, the turn continues. In the case of three or more homophonic forms, the player who draws the third form can play it on the matched pair already displayed and score two points, regardless of who has the matched pair.
2. In a like manner, directions can be altered so that the first player picks up a card, reads the word, and produces an appropriate sentence using the word. If correct, the card is laid aside as one point. If incorrectly used, the card is returned face down and the turn passes to the next player.
3. See Activity 10.10.

8.15 Abbreviation Matching Game (Intermediate)

Objective: To develop familiarity with abbreviations.

Materials: Deck of abbreviation cards for such abbreviations as the months of the year, days of the week, units of measure, and other common terms.

Directions: This game should have no more than four players in a group, although several groups may play simultaneously. Prepare a deck of abbreviation cards, with one card for the word and one card for the abbreviation of the word. Spread the cards out, face down. The first player picks a card and reads the word. He or she then takes another card to try to find a matching abbreviation. If the cards are a match, the player places the cards face up. If nonmatching cards are turned up, the cards are returned face down, and the turn passes to the next player. As long as the player can continue to match cards, the turn continues.

STUDY PROCEDURES

8.16 Crossword Spelling Puzzle (Intermediate)

Objective: To provide an enjoyable way of studying spelling words.

Materials: A spelling crossword puzzle.

Crossword Puzzle

Across

3. to wash in a tub (bath)
6. supreme ruler (king)
9. close to something (near)
10. opposite of small (large)
11. past tense of run (ran)
12. short personal letter (note)
14. to work for money (earn)
16. a strong smell (odor)
17. hospital worker (nurse)

Down

1. Fe_____ Fo Fum (fie)
2. an information card (sign)
4. capable (able)
5. man with courage (hero)
6. between thighs and feet (knees)
7. slender opening (narrow)
8. _____ Canyon (grand)
13. to posses an object (own)
15. what a hand is connected to (arm)

Directions: Prepare several spelling crossword puzzles such as shown in the sample. Let students work in pairs. Some sharing may be appropriate.

8.17 Spin-and-Spell Baseball (Primary or Intermediate)

Objective: To provide enjoyable practice with spelling.

Materials: Spelling baseball game board as illustrated, spelling cards, and score cards.

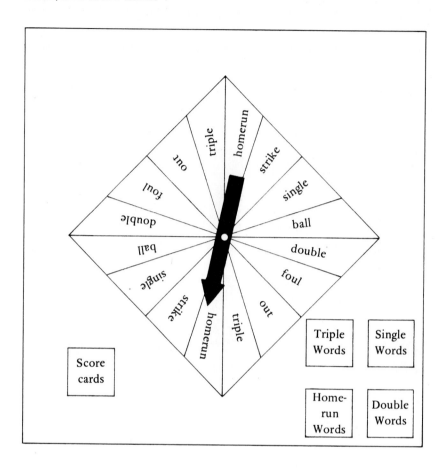

Directions: Separate the cards into the correct stacks—single, double, triple, homerun depending on difficulty of the word. Place each stack on the desk with the spelling words face down. Divide into two teams. Assign one person to be the score keeper and word caller. Decide which team will be at bat first. One person from this team will spin the dial on the game board. If the dial lands on a space marked single, double, triple, or home-run, the score keeper will pick the top card from the matching set of cards. The score keeper will pronounce the word aloud. The person at bat will then spell the word. If the spelling is correct, that person advances to the designated base. After the word has been pronounced, place it at the bottom of the stack. If "strike," "foul," "ball," or "out" is spun, no word is called; "out" retires the player, but "strike," "foul," and "ball" permit another spin (four "balls" is the equivalent of a "single"). The ground rules for this game are the same as for baseball. Three strikes constitute an out, three outs constitute a change of teams, and so forth. A point is scored for each run that is sent to home base.

At the end of a designated number of innings, the team with the most points wins.

8.18 Spelling Football (Primary or Intermediate, depending on words used)

Objective: To provide enjoyable practice in spelling.

Materials: Either a chalkboard and chalk or a sheet of unlined paper or poster board, felt-tip marker, index cards (with spelling words written on them), and small football-shaped cutout.

A football field is drawn on the chalkboard or on the unlined paper or poster board. The football cutout or a chalked X representing the football is placed at the fifty-yard line. The word cards are placed in a stack, face down.

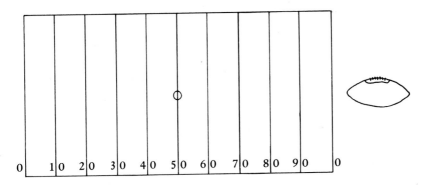

Directions: The game can be played by two students or two teams. The spelling cards are turned up one at a time by the referee. If the word is correctly spelled the football is advanced ten yards toward the goal, and the player(s) is allowed to try the next card. This procedure continues until there is a miss or until the ball reaches the goal line. If a miss occurs, the other player or team has a chance to spell the words and move the ball in the opposite direction. When the ball reaches the goal line, the player or team that is in control scores six points. This player or team is then allowed to spell another word to make the extra point. After the extra point is made or missed, the ball returns to the fifty-yard line with the opposing team in control.

PROOFREADING

8.19 Help a Friend Spell (Intermediate)

Objective: To provide practice in developing proofreading habits.

Materials: A worksheet such as follows.

Worksheet: Homophones

Review the meaning of these homophones:

> *your*   belongs to you, as in "your book"
> *you're*   you are, as in "You're a good student."
> *its*   belonging to it, as in "its foot"
> *it's*   it is, as in "It's raining."

Now help Joe correctly rewrite these sentences by correctly spelling the misspelled homophones.

1. "I know its you're coat," said David.
2. If your late, its you're own fault.
3. "Your sure it's tire is flat?" asked Norman.
4. "Is you're rabbit in it's cage?" asked Lynn.

Directions: The directions are provided on the worksheet.

DICTIONARY

The Alphabet

8.20 Pyramid Puzzle (Primary)

Objective: To provide practice with letters of the alphabet prior to dictionary work.

Materials: A pyramid puzzle, such as illustrated.

Directions: Ask the students to fill in the letters of the alphabet that match the numbers to make a word. Words are formed, making it a self-checking exercise.

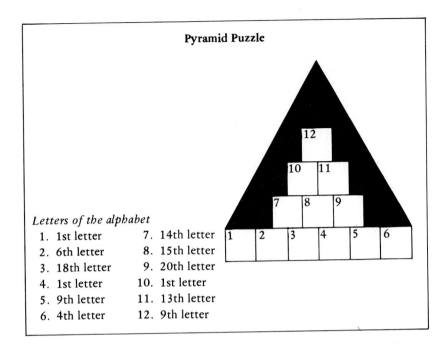

Pyramid Puzzle

Letters of the alphabet

1. 1st letter
2. 6th letter
3. 18th letter
4. 1st letter
5. 9th letter
6. 4th letter
7. 14th letter
8. 15th letter
9. 20th letter
10. 1st letter
11. 13th letter
12. 9th letter

Guide Words

8.21 Dictionary Road Signs (Intermediate)

Objective: To help students use guide words in searching the dictionary.

Materials: Ditto sheets as illustrated with lists of words.

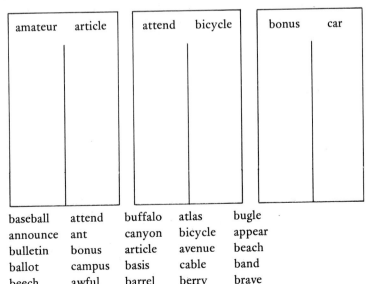

amateur	article	attend	bicycle	bonus	car

baseball	attend	buffalo	atlas	bugle
announce	ant	canyon	bicycle	appear
bulletin	bonus	article	avenue	beach
ballot	campus	basis	cable	band
beech	awful	barrel	berry	brave

Directions: Explain that the dictionary has guide words at the tops of pages. The student is to put the words on the correct page and then number the words in the order that they would appear. (Note: students need to know that the guide words at the top of a dictionary page tell them the first and last words on that page. If students are proficient in the use of alphabetical order, they should be able to decide whether or not a word will be found on a particular page by checking to see if the word alphabetically falls between the two guide words.)

Variations:
1. Students may form teams for this activity. When given a signal by the teacher, each group should begin to write the words which would be found on the pages illustrated. A time limit can be set for this part of the activity. Then the groups could arrange their words in alphabetical order on their dictionary pages. One point is given for each word that each group correctly lists for its pages. The group with the most points wins.
2. At a later time, papers with dictionary guide words only may be provided; students should write words which would be found on the dictionary page. Again, time limits may be set and points awarded for correct listings.

Dictionary Spelling Aid

8.22 Which Is Correct? (Intermediate)

Objective: To encourage student use of the dictionary when in doubt as to the spelling of a word.

Materials: Dictionary and list of words, such as the following:

1. which or wihch?
2. their or thier?
3. separate or seperate?
4. business or busness?
5. freind or friend?
6. since or sence?
7. woman or wimen?
8. writing or writting?
9. sure or shure?
10. Wednesday or Wedsday?
11. country or kuntry?
12. Feburary or February?
13. forty or fourty?
14. color or coler?

15. doctor or docter?   18. minut or minute?

16. whether or wether?   19. evry or every?

17. grammar or grammer?   20. truly or turly?

Directions: Ask students to consult the dictionary to determine the correct spelling of each of the words provided on the worksheet or chalkboard.

9 Handwriting

The primary purpose of handwriting is to express meaning. Students should have a purpose for writing, even in the earliest stages of instruction. Because handwriting is a skill, students will need practice and, at times, help and guidance from the teacher. But the basic motivation for improving their skill is a strong desire to express and to communicate. Accordingly, two of the four topics covered in this chapter are creating interest and developing greater legibility.

The other topics of this chapter are the two basic styles of handwriting: manuscript and cursive. Manuscript is a style of writing that uses simple curves and straight lines to produce unjoined letters. Cursive is a writing style in which the strokes of the letters are joined and the angles rounded. At the beginning of manuscript writing, chalkboards, easels, or large sheets of paper may be used. As skill increases, lined paper may be introduced for those who are coordinated enough to use it. The beginning space between lines is usually about one inch—some commercially available paper has a dotted or light-colored line as a guide for the height of lower-case letters. As teachers serve as models, it is important that their handwriting be firm, bold, and exact. Teachers who lack certainty and ease in manuscript writing should try to refine their skill.

The teacher should study the students' written work for clues to needs and should provide practice for overcoming troublesome letters. The teacher often works with small groups on several different writing tasks and gives individuals help when needed. Teachers should closely observe the students as they begin developing handwriting skills and check that proper habits are established—such as appropriate holding of chalk or pencil, correct placement for right- and for left-handed pupils, and convenient desk height. Some common errors in manuscript must be given special attention: incorrect size (particularly descenders), reversal problems (*d, b, q, g, s, y*), and addition to letters (*m, U, I, q, C, k, y*), incorrect relationship to parts of letters (*k, R, M, m*), and incorrect placement of letters relative to the line.

Not all pupils will be ready at the same time to move from manuscript to cursive; some will be ready by the middle of the second grade; others should wait until the latter part of the third grade or even the beginning of the fourth. Evidence of *readiness* includes the ability to write manuscript letters well from memory, the ability to read cursive writing, and a desire to learn cursive writing. During the transitional period, the students may continue to use manuscript writing for some work, especially that done without the close supervision of the teacher.

Pen work should be introduced only when the pupils are capable of writing acceptably with a pencil. For some pupils, this may mean grade four; for others, grade five. The fountain pen is useful, but the ball point pen is favored by many.

Again, some common error patterns in cursive writing should be given special attention: failure to close letters, closing looped strokes (*l* and *e*), looping nonlooped strokes (*i*), and straight-up strokes rather than rounded strokes (*n, c, h*). The arabic numerals 5, 0, and 2 are most often written illegibly. Often it is not individual letter formation but letter combinations that cause difficulty, especially letters followed by *e, i, o, r,* or *y*. Cooperatively developed teacher-pupil charts are helpful in summarizing special points to check in cursive writing. Proper habits should be established for right- and for left-handed writers in regard to correct paper placement, appropriate holding of chalk or pencil, and convenient desk height.

In all phases of manuscript and cursive handwriting, the perceptual-motor nature of learning should be emphasized. This means that primary focus should be upon helping students build mental perception of letters and their formation as a guide for motor practice. Images of the letter form are achieved through many exposures to the formation of letters, oral description of the process of letter formation, self-correction by comparison, and consistent letter-form models.

A handwriting learning center should be supplied with suitable instruments, materials, and activity ideas. These should include individual pupil folders, handwriting evaluation sheets and checklists, copies of the alphabet (upper and lower case and the numerals), a skill file of handwriting pages, file cards describing letter formations, a file of activity cards stressing the different strokes and features of letters, a set of large tracing cards, a file of "Special Handwriting Activities," various handwriting charts, and pencils, ball points, chalk, and the like.

A special effort will be required to maintain interest in handwriting. Handwriting periods should be varied rather than follow a routine pattern. Some lessons will be functional, others will involve analysis and practice, and some will deal with the historical development of handwriting. Because handwriting is a skill that is used in all other curricular areas, attention should be given to it as needed throughout the school day. Special handwriting periods are usually necessary for students to reach and maintain the desired efficiency, but instruction and practice should be based on the needs of students in practical writing situations. Other suggestions that may prove useful in adding interest to handwriting lessons include: use of the opaque projector or the overhead transparency to analyze handwriting, rating handwriting in work done in the other content areas, making charts, giving suggestions for handwriting, display of pupils' handwriting on bulletin boards, study of various handwriting tools and various styles of writing, rating papers by someone outside the classroom, and providing an atmosphere of interest and respect for good handwriting.

Finally handwriting needs to be evaluated. While there are standardized merit scales, informal devices should be used for determining quality in handwriting and locating specific weaknesses. The most important criterion for evaluating handwriting is its legibility. Speed is also important but should not be stressed to where it interferes with legibility. Letter formation is the chief factor affecting legibility, but spacing, alignment, slant, and line quality must also be taken into account.

MANUSCRIPT

A Multisensory Approach

9.1 Salt Writing (Primary)

Objective: To utilize sensory awareness during letter formation in manuscript writing.

Materials: A number of flat trays, box of salt, and a poster board with lines.

Directions: Make a model of each student's name on strips of lined poster board. Demonstrate how to write a name in salt which has been poured on a tray. In groups of five or six, seat students with trays on a table of appropriate height. Pour a mound of salt on each tray or allow students to pour. Demonstrate each student's name in his or her own tray. Shake the salt to erase.

After several writings of the name, check to see which students are having difficulty with which letters. Provide more exercise for those. For variety, use another material on other days—coarse sand, flour, rice.

9.2 Fingerpaint Writing (Primary)

Objective: To stimulate writing readiness through sensory awareness.

Materials: Fingerpaint paper and fingerpaint.

Directions: Provide students with paper and paint. Show them a clock face and ask them to begin where the numeral 2 should be and make a clock face on their paper. Repeat with various other shapes, such as doughnuts, balls, soap bubbles, until the students can easily make smooth circles.

9.3 Making Letters (Primary)

Objective: To utilize concrete objects to stimulate sensory awareness related to manuscript writing.

Materials: Life savers (for circles), toothpicks (for straight lines), pieces of yarn (cut in short lengths for the curves), and small beans or seeds (for dots).

Directions: Provide several pieces of the above materials for each student. Place large models of each lower-case manuscript letter in the chalktray. Ask the students to make as many letters as they can from the materials provided. Discuss the letters formed in terms of circles, straight lines, and curves. Short, familiar words can be formed with these same materials, and a sentence or message may be composed.

Legibility

9.4 What's Easy and Difficult? (Primary or Intermediate; manuscript or cursive)

Objective: To help students identify their problem letter and to provide practice in refining these letters.

Materials: Bulletin board display.

What's Easy? What's Difficult?

1. Which letter is easiest for you to write?
2. Which letter is hardest for you to write?
3. Write a sentence. Be sure it contains your "easiest" letter.
4. Write a sentence. Make sure it contains your "most difficult" letter.
5. Write this sentence as carefully as you can; make your "most difficult" letter the best you can.

The quick brown fox jumped over the lazy dogs.

Directions: The directions are provided on the bulletin board. This activity may be used for either manuscript or cursive.

9.5 Improve Your *g*'s (Primary)

Objective: To provide individual assistance in improving manuscript letter formation.

Materials: Worksheet, as suggested:

Worksheet: Manuscript *g*

Write this word. How does *g* look?

good

Look at how *g* is made.
1. Which part is made first?
2. Which way do you move your pencil to make the circle?
3. How wide is the lower part?
4. Where does it finish?

Making *g*'s in these boxes should help you. Then make good *g*'s without the boxes.

Look at *g, j,* and *q.*
   1. Which two letters end alike?
   2. How are *g* and *q* different?
   3. Make *g, j,* and *q.*

Make good *g*'s as you write these words.

Write this sentence. Are you making good *g*'s?

Are you making better *g*'s?
   1. Are you moving your pencil the right way to make the circle?
   2. Is the lower part as wide as the circle?
   3. Does the lower part end high enough?

Directions: Provide a copy of the self-directed worksheet to students who need it. Discuss the material with them. Similar worksheets may be prepared for other letters and for other aspects such as alignment, slant, and spacing.

9.6 Use All Letters! (Primary or Intermediate; manuscript or cursive)

Objective: To utilize student self-checking in ascertaining and remediating writing difficulties.

Materials: Paper and pencil and a worksheet as illustrated:

Worksheet: Check Your Writing

If you write the practice sentence below you will be using all twenty-six letters! Write it in your spare time today and compare your copy with this one. Check letter formation, size and height of letter, spacing alignment, and slant. Talk with me about your best and poorest points.

The quick brown fox jumped over the lazy dogs.

Manuscript:

_____

_____

Cursive:

_____

_____

_____

Directions: The directions are provided on the worksheet. This activity may be used for either manuscript or cursive.

Motivation

9.7 Bear Letters (Primary)

Objective: To highlight correct manuscript letter sizes.

Materials: A bulletin board as illustrated.

Directions: In using this bulletin board, talk about the story "The Three Little Bears" and compare their sizes. Then try to get the students to tell which letter (*i, t, l*) is tallest, shortest, medium-sized. Label the letters with word cards (short, medium, tall). Generate a list of words beginning with *i, t, l* by brainstorming. Challenge the students to show how well they could make those letters as they write the words. After the students have practiced and evaluated their papers, mount them in open spaces on the bulletin board.

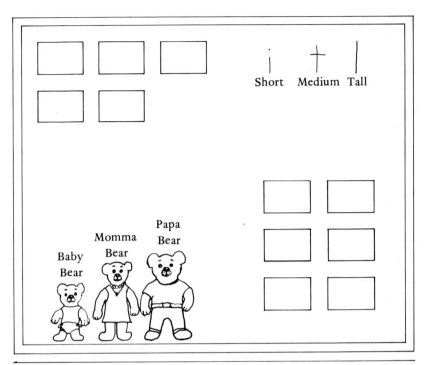

9.8 Write a New Headline (Intermediate)

Objective: To provide a motivational situation for utilizing spacing, height relationships, and manuscript letter formation.

Materials: Bulletin board display.

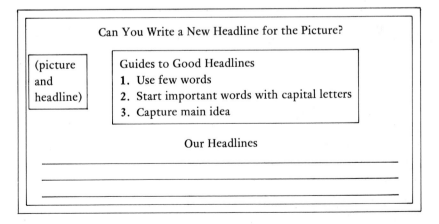

Directions: Discuss the purposes of a headline: to make people want to read a news story; to give information in a nutshell; to serve as a title for the picture. Call attention to qualities of a good headline, such as stated on the illustrated bulletin board. Ask students to compose several headlines on practice paper and choose their best one to write in their best handwriting on lined paper to be posted on the bulletin board under the picture.

CURSIVE

9.9 Word Match (Primary)

Objective: To assist recognition of letters and words written in both manuscript and cursive.

Materials: Index cards (3″ × 5″): two sets, one with words written in manuscript, one with the same words written in cursive.

Directions: Students may work in pairs. Place the cursive set of cards face down on a table or on the floor. Place the manuscript set to the right or left of the first in the same manner. Each player takes three cards from each pile. Then, they toss a coin to decide who goes first. The first player turns over a card from the manuscript set; if the card matches a cursive card in the player's hand, the player places them at the side and repeats the procedure with the cursive set. If they do not match, the player replaces them in their original position and the next player takes a turn. Play continues until all cards have been matched.

Variations:
1. To simplify, ask the students to match a manuscript letter with its equivalent cursive letter. Or a series of two or three manuscript letters may be matched to the same series of two or three cursive letters.
2. An individual student can use the cards as practice in making the association of manuscript and cursive letters or words.
3. Students may be given only one form—manuscript or cursive—and asked to write the corresponding form.

Legibility

9.10 Be a Handwriting Detective (Intermediate)

Objective: To provide practice in forming cursive letters.

Materials: Writing paper and pencil for students, chalkboard and chalk for teacher, lower- and upper-case cursive letters, numbered as shown.

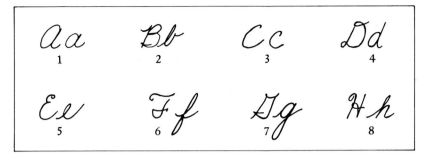

Directions: Prepare the chalkboard or bulletin board display as suggested above. Give directions, such as "Write the letters number 19, 5, 1. Can you make a word using these letters?" Call out the numbers that represent the name of a student in the classroom. Call out a set of numbers and ask, "How many words can you make from these letters?"

9.11 Watch the Ovals (Intermediate)

Objective: To provide practice on certain oval letters, such as *a, c, d, g, o,* and *q.*

Materials: Bulletin board display.

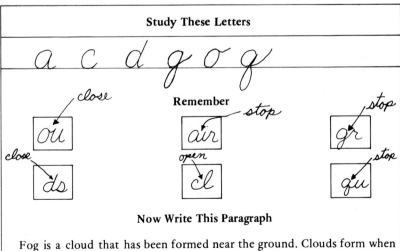

Study These Letters

Remember

Now Write This Paragraph

Fog is a cloud that has been formed near the ground. Clouds form when warm moist air rises and meets a layer of cooler air. It can happen quite often.

Directions: The students should study the special points to remember which are posted on the bulletin board. Then they should go to the writing center, where paper and pencil are provided. They practice on the specific examples provided on the bulletin board. Then they write the paragraph, paying close attention to the formation of oval letters.

9.12 Eight-Letter Game (Intermediate)

Objective: To provide practice with lower-case cursive writing.

Materials: Pencils and paper and twenty-six index cards (with words beginning with the different letters of the alphabet).

Directions: Tell the students to write any eight letters they choose on a sheet of paper, one per line. Shuffle the twenty-six cards. Then turn the cards over, one at a time, and reveal them to the students. When students see the word, they write the word next to the proper beginning letter, if they have it on their paper.

Variations:
1. The same activity could be used with manuscript letter forms.
2. The same activity could be utilized, focusing upon the *last* letter of the word or with the third letter in the word.

9.13 Too Many *P*'s (Intermediate)

Objective: To provide practice with the cursive letter *p*—upper and lower case.

Materials: Copy of a tongue twister or selection with many *p*'s.
A Peck of Pickled Peppers
Peter Piper picked a peck of pickled peppers.
A peck of pickled peppers Peter Piper picked.
If Peter Piper picked a peck of pickled peppers,
Where's the peck of pickled peppers Peter Piper picked?

Directions: Ask the students to copy the tongue twister or appropriate selection carefully. Ask them to compare their copy with the one on the chalkboard (or displayed on the bulletin board), by answering questions such as the following:

1. Are all your lower-case *p*'s the same height?
2. Are all your upper-case *P*'s the same height?
3. Are the shapes of your *p*'s or *P*'s the same as those on the copy?
4. Do all your *p*'s sit on the lines and come the same distance below the baseline?

Variations:
1. Other letters can be utilized in a similar manner.
2. Shorter tongue twisters can be used. For example, "Round and round the rugged rock, the ragged rascal ran."

9.14 Improve your *e*'s (Intermediate)

Objective: To utilize self-evaluation in improving cursive letter formation.

Materials: Worksheet.

Worksheet: cursive *e*

Write this word and see how well you made *e*.

east

Look at how *e* is made.
   1. Where does *e* begin?
   2. Do you have a good loop in *e*?
   3. Where do the lines cross to form the loop?

Make *e*'s between these lines and then try making good *e*'s without the lines.

Look at the word mile.
   1. How are *e* and *l* different?
   2. How are *e* and *i* different?
   3. If *e* is made too tall, what would the word look like?
   4. Write the word *mile*.

Make good *e*'s as you write these words.

letter   ever   deep

sleep   smile   wheel

See how well you can write this sentence. Then look at the *e*'s. How do they look?

Tell them to keep quiet!

Are you making better *e*'s?
1. Do you have loops in all *e*'s?
2. Do any *e*'s look like *l*'s? Be sure they don't.
3. Do any *e*'s look like *i*'s? If they do, what do you need to do?

Directions: Provide a copy of the self-directed worksheet to students who need further practice. Discuss the material with them. Similar worksheets may be prepared for other letters and for other aspects such as alignment, slant, spacing.

Motivation

9.15 Writing Horoscopes! (Intermediate)

Objective: To provide motivation for cursive handwriting activity.

Materials: The twelve zodiac signs, pencils and writing paper, drawing paper and crayons.

Directions: Display the twelve zodiac sign posters. Discuss each student's sign and horoscopes in general. Provide art materials for students to make their own individual sign. Encourage the students to walk around and observe signs of other class members. Then a student picks a partner and pretends to see the future, neatly writing out the partner's horoscope for the week. After completion, each partner switches horoscopes to read. These may be read to the class or displayed on the bulletin board along with the matching zodiac poster.

Variation: Other motivational handwriting situations abound. For example, a student with a birthday can be made to feel very special by receiving greeting cards made by classmates. Such cards can be composed of sayings, poems, riddles, letters, or notes.

9.16 Researching Handwriting Topics (Intermediate)

Objective: To create interest and motivation through exploration of different handwriting styles and materials.

Materials: Trade books and reference books, set of ideas for researching, such as "How Pencils Are Made," "Story of the Alphabet," "Indian Picture Writing," "Our Writing Tools and How We Got Them," "History of Handwriting."

Directions: Provide trade books and reference books that deal with handwriting history. Ask students to choose a topic of interest, research it, and plan a way to share their findings with others. Encourage interesting methods of presentation such as developing a filmstrip about handwriting with an accompanying story. Some titles that may be helpful include:

Cahn, William, and Rhoda Cahn. *The Story of Writing*. Irvington-on-Hudson, New York: Harvey House, 1963.

Dugan, William. *How Our Alphabet Grew*. New York: Golden, 1972.

Epstein, Samuel, and Beryl Epstein. *The First Book of Printing*. New York: Franklin Watts, Inc., 1955.

Gourdie, Tom. *The Puffin Book of Lettering*. Baltimore: Penguin Books, 1961.

Hofsinde, Robert (Gray-Wolf). *Indian Picture Writing*. New York: William Morrow and Co., 1959.

Irwin, Keith Gordon. *The Romance of Writing*. New York: Viking, 1957.

McCain, Murray. *Writing*. New York: Farrar, Strauss, and Giroux, 1964.

Ogg, Oscar. *The Twenty-Six Letters*, rev. ed. New York: Thomas Y. Crowell, 1971.

Russell, Solvey Paulson. *A Is for Apple and Why: Story of Our Alphabet*. New York: Abingdon Press, 1959.

Scott, Joseph, and Lenore Scott. *Heiroglyphs for Fun*. New York: Van Nostrand Reinhold, 1974.

10 Vocabulary Development

The medium of language is words, whether they are read or written, spoken or heard, and communication depends on the manipulation of words. Each word has a functional purpose or a meaning, at least to the person who is trying to communicate. Consequently vocabulary development, the learning of words, must be a vital element of the language arts curriculum.

In promoting vocabulary growth, several benefits are derived. Each time a student acquires a new word and its related concept, the student's store of knowledge is increased. This enriches the student's basic learning as well as increases the ability to communicate with language. Also, each new word serves as a vehicle for countless concepts which may be built around the knowledge of that word. For example, if a student learns what the word *jipijapa* means, a whole new learning has begun: the student will be introduced to a unique plant, given some information about Central and South America, informed of some potential uses of plants that are uncommon in the United States, told something of the biological nature of tropical plants, given a mental picture of an unusual element of nature, informed of some differences between the English and Spanish pronunciations of vowels and consonants, and will have gained some insight into one of the artistic fashions of Panama!

This chapter emphasizes these topics: (1) words are vehicles intended to convey meaning or concepts; (2) special categories of words are formed according to meanings or purpose; (3) words can convey images and feelings; and (4) semantics is the study of meaning in language.

The activities in the first section of the chapter are intended to develop the students' awareness of the relation between words and their meanings and the concepts they represent. Activities focus on the relating of words to topics, the introduction of multisyllabic words, and the developing of the ability to "picture" word meanings; activities also provide experience in using concept-related words, the dictionary, and discovering word analogies.

The second part of this chapter provides activities for special categories of words. It is very beneficial for students to view words in relation to other words. When they are grouping words to be put in their own "dictionaries," students are weighing each word in terms of its own meaning and its relation to the larger category. Activities in this section deal with prefixes, homonyms, synonyms, heteronyms, and figurative expression.

The ability to use words expressively is an art which also may be taught in the classroom. The appropriate selection of words which are accurately descriptive or intriguingly creative is not an easy task. Instruction in word selection should thus increase the students' familiarity with language and the power of words. Accordingly, the third set of activities promotes the use of descriptive words, "color" words, more specific words, sensory words, and the use of the thesaurus.

The last set of activities in this chapter involves the concept of semantics—the study of meaning in language. Within this section the activities explore the concepts of understanding referents (multiple meaning of words), euphemisms, slang expressions, technical language, and affective language.

WORD MEANINGS AND CONCEPTS

10.1 Relate the Words (Primary)

Objective: To illustrate the relationship between words and concepts.

Materials: Construction paper, scissors, felt-tip marker, and dictionary (optional, thesaurus).

Primary

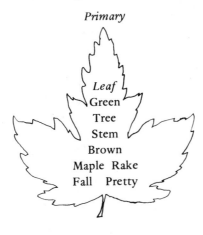

Leaf
Green
Tree
Stem
Brown
Maple Rake
Fall Pretty

Directions: Select words which can be identified by a picture. (Some items that are appropriate include clothes, food, animals, cars, seashells.) These words are then illustrated by cutout construction paper. Students then write on the construction paper any related words.

Variation: Older students may participate in the same activity but with more advanced concepts and words.

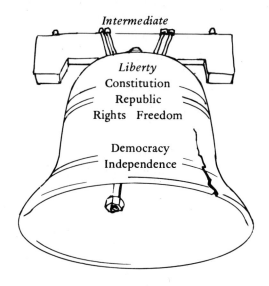

10.2 Word Pictures (Primary)

Objective: To allow students to have fun in visually associating words and meanings.

Materials: Examples of pictured words.

corner   circle   tent

Directions: Ask the students to list words that can be pictured in a way to reveal their meaning. (Additional words can be suggested by the teacher.) Then the students draw or construct these words in such a way as to illustrate each word's meaning.

Variations:

1. Older students may be instructed to use words with which they are presently unfamiliar.
2. Students may also construct word pictures and have their classmates guess what the word is.

10.3 Acrostic-You-Crossed-It (Intermediate)

Objective: To stimulate students to discover concept-related vocabulary terms.

Materials: Several laminated problem cards with words written vertically on them, clue card, and solution card.

Problem Card

```
  - - - N - -
  - - - - - A
  P - - - -
  - - O - - - - - -
  - - - - L -
    - E - - - -
  - - - - - O -
  - - N - - - - -
```

Clue Card

N Emperor of the _____
A Foolishly attacked _____ in winter
P His personality
O His self-centeredness
L He frequently planned strategies for _____
E Eventually he suffered a crushing _____
O The end of his empire came at _____
N Desired to be _____ of the world

Solution Card

```
  F R E N C H
R U S S I A
    P R O U D
    E G O C E N T R I C
B A T T L E
      D E F E A T
W A T E R L O O
    C O N Q U E R O R
```

Directions: Students are given a laminated card with a vertically printed word on it and are given clues (either orally or reproduced on a clue card.) The clues should describe, define, or explain the problem word. Answers may be checked by the solution card.

10.4 Dictionary Hunt (Primary or Intermediate)

Objective: To provide students with experience in searching for various elements found in the dictionary.

Materials: A dictionary (the same edition for each student of each team and appropriate for their age level). A worksheet with set of questions with the dictionary page number on which the answers can be found.

Worksheet: Dictionary Hunt

Find:

1. A word that has four *syllables* (p.   )
2. A word that means the same as *mammal* (p.   )
3. A word that rhymes with *see* (p.   )
4. A word that has a *schwa sound* in it (p.   )
5. A word that has *two different spellings* (p.   )
6. A word that is *accented* on the third syllable (p.   )
7. A word that has *no plural form* (p.   )
8. A word that represents something you *can eat* (p.   )
9. A word that is derived from a *Latin word* (p.   )
10. A word that is *no longer used* (p.   )
11. A word that can be pronounced two different ways but has the same spelling for both pronunciations (p.   )
12. A word that serves as an *interjection* (p.   )
13. A word with an *affix* (p.   )
14. A word that should be *capitalized* (p.   )
15. A word which has a unique usage in a *special field* (for example, biology, law, theology) (p.   )

Directions: The teacher passes out to each student or team the set of questions. The student or team which correctly identifies the most words at the end of the game is declared "Dictionary Detective of the Day."

Variations:

1. Students may make up their set of questions and trade with other students.
2. To direct attention to dictionary usage for one element (word meanings) other kinds of worksheets can be developed:

Would you like to eat at a *curio*? Why or why not?
Would you like to be an *equestrian*? Why or why not?
Would you like to own an *antique*? Why or why not?

10.5 Analogy Write-Up! (Intermediate)

Objective: To provide practice in relating words through similarity of various kinds.

Materials: Eleven sheets of poster board.

Analogy Techniques

Type	Example
1. Antonyms	1. *strong* is to *weak* as *up* is to _____.
2. Synonyms	2. *happy* is to *glad* as *sad* is to _____.
3. Homonyms	3. *see* is to *sea* as *sew* is to _____.
4. Origin/result	4. *cow* is to *beef* as *pig* is to _____.
5. Singular/plural	5. *man* is to *men* as *woman* is to _____.
6. Part/whole	6. *toe* is to *foot* as *finger* is to _____.
7. Object/function	7. *apple* is to *eat* as *pencil* is to _____.
8. Ratio	8. *one* is to *four* as *two* is to _____.
9. Class/member	9. *cardinal* is to *bird* as *Dalmation* is to _____.
10. Degree	10. *tall* is to *taller* as *short* is to _____.

Directions: On one poster board, write the label "Analogy Techniques." Put one example for each type. Discuss the types and example.

On the other sheets of poster board, put an example of a different analogy type and label each one. Display the ten posters on the bulletin board. Ask the students to write an example of each of the analogy types. The class members share the examples they have written and receive feedback concerning their accuracy.

SPECIAL CATEGORIES OF WORDS

10.6 Root Word Wheel (Primary)

Objective: To illustrate the relationship of words to their root words.

Materials: Poster board, scissors, felt-tip markers, word wheel, as shown.

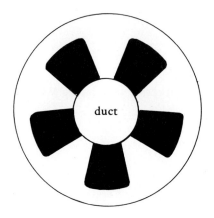

Directions: Cut out of the posterboard the basic framework of a wheel with the hub and spokes. In the center, put a root word. The students are to add various *prefixes* (*ab-, de-, con-, in-, pro-*) to the spokes.

10.7 Homonym Hunt (Intermediate)

Objective: To provide practice in recognition of homonyms.

Materials: Chalkboard and chalk, dictionary for each student, list of words on the chalkboard.

not	pair	whole	steal
beat	made	tied	pain
sail	piece	led	weight
fourth	waste	fare	hair

Directions: Instruct the students to locate homonyms for the words listed on the board, using their dictionaries if necessary. (Identical phonetic respellings indicate homonyms.) Then ask them to write a sentence containing each homonym. After they complete this list, they may search for other homonyms not on the list.

10.8 Synonym Tree (Primary)

Objective: To provide practice in identifying words with similar meanings.

Materials: Poster board, felt-tip pens, thumb tacks, scissors, and word cards.

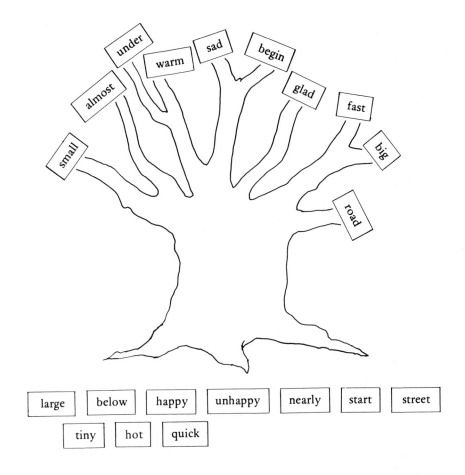

Directions: Draw a tree on the poster board. Attach word cards to the tree. Explain that "matching" cards that belong on the tree have fallen off. Ask the students to put them where they belong.

Variations:
1. This activity could be used by two students or a small instructional group. Several trees and word cards could be made with no words and children could make up their own synonym words.
2. See Activity 10.9.

10.9 Synonym Search (Intermediate)

Objectives: To familiarize students with synonyms and to begin a synonym file.

Materials: An index-card file, dictionary, thesaurus, and an introductory set of words such as the following,

good	pretty	sad
happy	nice	set
mean	cute	high
ugly	walk	still
bad	go	real

Directions: Basic words or concepts are identified. Students are to find synonyms for these words. The basic word is written on a tab; all synonyms are written on an index card, along with the synonym's definition, and placed behind the basic word in the file.

Variations:
1. Students may also include in their synonym cards words which are related but not synonyms.
2. Phrases or expressions may also be included in addition to words.
3. Two thesaurus references are:
Schiller, Andrew, and William Jenkins. *In Other Words: A Beginning Thesaurus.* New York: Lothrop, 1978; and their *In Other Words: A Junior Thesaurus.* New York: Lothrop, 1978.

10.10 Antonym Dominoes (Intermediate)

Objective: To provide practice in identifying antonyms.

Materials: Index cards marked with two sections. Write one word on each side using a magic marker. The basic set will include these cards. (Others may be added by students or teacher.)

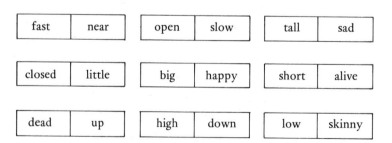

fast	near		open	slow		tall	sad
closed	little		big	happy		short	alive
dead	up		high	down		low	skinny

sour	night	wet	sweet	rough	dry

before	far	dirty	wrong	over	right

cold	under	story	off	bottom	go

dark	hot	light	smooth	top	good

bad	poor	rich	after	day	fat

Directions: This game is to be played with two or four players. Each player is dealt two cards. One card is put face up in the playing area. The player who can match a word on one of his or her cards to its antonym on the exposed card goes first. Play proceeds clockwise. Each player, in turn, tries to match one of his or her words with an antonym of it in the playing area. If the player has no match, he or she may draw one card. If there is still no match, go on to the next player. One point is earned for each antonym matched. Cards may extend in any direction, so long as the word on one card touches its antonym on the other card. When all the cards have been played, the student with the most points wins.

Variation: Similar games may be played with synonyms and homonyms. Words on cards may be varied according to vocabulary and reading level of students.

10.11 How Many Meanings? (Intermediate)

Objective: To help students understand the multimeanings of words.

Materials: Duplicating master, typewriter or pen, dictionaries, list of multimeaning words.

can	turn	run
change	head	bark
cut	left	sharp
kind	light	mouth
like	mean	strike
book	over	miss

Directions: Distribute copies of the list of multimeaning words to the students. Instruct them to search the dictionaries for meanings and to write a separate sentence for each meaning. Have a class discussion of the answers.

Variation: Let students take the list home to search for meanings and to write sentences with parents and other resource people as sources of information.

10.12 Crossword Similars (Intermediate)

Objective: To develop students' ability to identify and to distinguish between homonyms and heteronyms.

Materials: Graph or grid paper which can be used to make up a crossword puzzle and a list of homonyms and heteronyms.

Homonyms	Heteronyms
sum	row
some	row
to	bow
two	bow
too	
	read
pen	read
pin	
	lives
ten	lives
tin	

Down
1. He _____ in a green house.
4. May I have _____ of your candy?
5. He _____ this book.

Across
2. A cat has nine _____ .
3. When you add two numbers you get a _____ .
6. She will _____ aloud to the class.

Directions: The students list brief descriptions that distinguish the words and that can be used as crossword puzzle meanings. A crossword puzzle is constructed by each student. Students then trade and work their classmates' puzzles.

Variation: Rather than working a crossword puzzle, students may try to think of as many homonym and heteronym pairs as possible.

They score one point for each pair listed and one point for labeling the pair correctly as either homonyms or heteronyms. First person or team to reach twenty-five points wins; alternately, the team with the most points after fifteen minutes wins.

10.13 Let's Race to the Moon—Figuratively Speaking, of Course! (Intermediate)

Objective: To develop students' ability to identify and to use figurative speech, idioms, and homonyms in their everyday language.

Materials: Two moon charts.

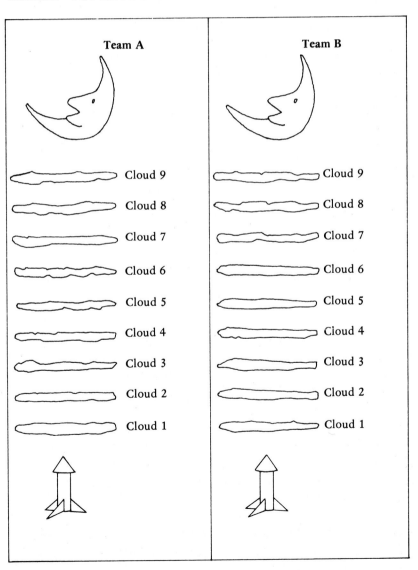

Directions: Students are divided into two teams. The object is to race the rocket to the moon; the game is over after the round following Cloud 9. Students from both teams are given three minutes to come up with an idiom, a homonym, or figurative speech. Following the time limit each group acts out or draws a literal interpretation of their sentence. For example, "She was frightened and turned a little pale (pail)"

and "He couldn't carry a tune in a bucket."

After each successful round the rocket is moved up one cloud.

Variations:
1. This activity may be played as a relay, with individuals being singly responsible for the idioms, homonyms, or figurative speech.
2. The activity need not be competitive nor timed.

WORDS FOR EXPRESSION

10.14 A-B-C Slide-a-Word (Primary or Intermediate)

Objectives: To illustrate the grammatical function of descriptive words.

Materials: Several long strips of blank poster board and several long strips of poster board with various simple sentences—spaced as shown—written horizontally on them; a second strip of poster board should be glued to the back with unglued spaces forming slots for the vertical strips to slide through. Double slits should be left for word panels to show through.

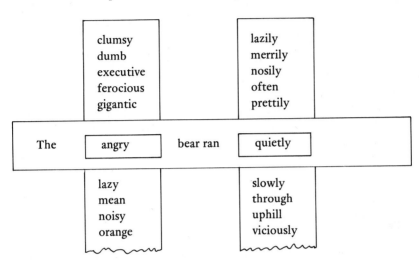

Directions: On blank strips of poster board the students are to write vertically words which start with each letter of the alphabet. The words all must serve the function of the missing word in the sentence; for example, all must be adjectives or adverbs. After all the words have been written down on the poster board, the students go through and read the possible sentence combinations. They then sort out the sentences and write them under such category headings as Humorous, Unusual, Mysterious, Sad, Impossible, Joyful.

Variation: Open sentences with only functional words may be used. The students must replace all the words so they would fit the structure of the sentence.

10.15 "Coloring and Mooding" Your Writing (Intermediate)

Objective: To provide students with experiences in identifying and categorizing words (or phrases) which provide mood or tone color to writing.

Materials: A notebook, a dictionary, list of such categories for notebook entries as

Words or phrases of sadness
Words or phrases of joy
Words or phrases of pain
Words or phrases of surprise
Words or phrases of beauty
Words or phrases of mystery, intrigue, or suspense
Words or phrases of color
Picturesque words or phrases

Directions: Students are instructed to put a category title on the top of a page in their notebooks. Every time a word or phrase of particular appeal is found to pertain to a specific category, the students are to write the word or phrase down on that page. All of these categories are continually expanded, and new categories can be added. Students are encouraged to avoid common or predictable expression or words.

Variation: For younger children, pictures can be pasted on the category pages which deal with that category. The primary student should then be able to tell about each picture and what the picture has to do with the category.

10.16 Use Specific Words (Primary)

Objective: To provide practice with using more specific words.

Materials: A sample passage and a list of alternate words.

Three people were playing when they heard something. They went to see what it was. They saw a boy going up a tree. They said, "What was the sound?" He said, "It was a bird."

little girls, asked, a loud sound, climbing, jumping rope, noise, answered, bluejay, hurried

Directions: Prepare a passage as cited above with a list of alternate words. Ask the students to replace the underlined words with more specific words supplied beneath the passage: Discuss after completion.

10.17 Words About Senses (Primary)

Objective: To provide practice with sensory words.

Materials: Bulletin board as indicated.

Sense Words	
Tasting Words	sour
Seeing Words	green
Feeling Words	glad
Hearing Words	rattle
Smelling Words	lemon
W o r d s	

Directions: Prepare a bulletin board as illustrated. Provide words to insert in containers at the bottom of the bulletin board. Pupils tack them up in the appropriate places.

Variation: The classification activity could involve various categories and the appropriate words.

Animal, Vegetable, Mineral Words
People Words
Sports Words
Hobby Words
Newspaper Words
Television Words

10.18 Thesaurus Questions (Intermediate)

Objective: To familiarize students with the thesaurus.

Materials: Chalkboard and chalk and a sample entry from a thesaurus, as illustrated.

Entry word	*say* (v)	Say means to express in words.
Synonyms	*order*	If you give a command, you have given an order.
	demand	Demand means to ask for urgently. Joe and Jim demand their turn.
	shout	Shout means to exclaim in a loud voice. His shout could be heard for blocks.
	advise	Advise means to inform. Sarah will advise you of her plans.
	remark	Remarks mean comments or statements. Bill's remarks gave away his true feelings.

Directions: Draw a large facsimile of the sample thesaurus page on the chalkboard. Divide the class into two teams. Ask pertinent questions about the information represented by the entry. Direct the first question to Team A. If Team A's representative answers correctly, Team A gets a point and Team B is asked a new question. If Team A's representative answers incorrectly, Team B has an opportunity to answer. If Team B's representative answers correctly, that team gets two points. If Team B's representative fails to answer correctly, the teacher gives the answer and Team A is given a new question.

Sample Questions:
1. What words are synonyms of *say*?
2. Why would *shout* be a better word than *say* to describe an angry statement?
3. Which sentence illustrates how *demand* is used?
4. When would it be more exact to use *shout* instead of *say*?

SEMANTICS

10.19 Which Meaning? (Primary)

Objective: To help students determine the appropriate meaning of a multiple-meaning word.

Materials: Poster board, paper fasteners, yarn, and a felt-tip pen.

Strike

Meanings			*Persons*
1. stop work	○	○	1. batter
2. a missed swing at a ball	○	○	2. fisherman
3. tell the time	○	○	3. boxer
4. many blows	○	○	4. clock repair
5. to hook a fish	○	○	5. worker

Directions: At the top of the sheet of poster board, write a multiple-meaning word. Then write different meanings of the word in one column; list persons often using each of the different meanings in an opposite column. Attach paper fasteners beside each meaning and each sentence as shown in the example.

Cut lengths of yarn long enough to reach from number 1 in the first column to number 5 in the second column with at least one inch to spare. Tie a length of yarn to each paper fastener in the first column.

Write the answers to the activity on the back side of the poster board.

Place the poster board in a learning center with direction to the students to match each meaning with the person for which that meaning is often used by connecting meanings and sentences with the lengths of yarn. The loose ends of the yarn can be looped around the paper fasteners. The students can self-check by looking at the answers on the back.

10.20 Euphemism Search (Intermediate)

Objective: To provide practice in identifying and interpreting figures of speech.

Materials: Multiple copies of a story containing many euphemisms.

Worksheet: Euphemisms

Underline the euphemisms. Think of a literal meaning for each one.

Career Opportunities

Hershel left the farm to find employment. He was underprivileged, and the recent recession had liquidated his assets. The farm alone did not make enough income to get Hershel out of the red. So he secured all the doors and windows and headed to the nearest metropolis to seek his fame and fortune.

He was not content with the city. The mass transit system was always tardy, and the restaurants were not affordable. All the buildings were antiques and much of the city was undergoing urban renewal. But Hershel went to find work.

The first job he procured was as a custodian in a senior citizens' convalescent home. He resigned after a week because the foreman was mentally unsound. His next job was in a funeral parlor as a sanitary engineer. It was a temporary position and Hershel wasn't keen about working around morticians and people who had passed away. But as he was hunting for another job, a police officer took him into custody in a case of mistaken identity.

Directions: Review with the class the idea of euphemisms. Then distribute the copies of the story. The students should be instructed to locate as many euphemisms as they can and then give a literal meaning for each one. A time limit may be set, or the teacher may allow the students to work until everyone has finished. A student scores a point for each euphemism located and another point for each correct alternate word.

Variation: Types of figures of speech may be categorized, with students being asked to draw pictures representing each of them or to explain them.

Figures of resemblance
Allegory—"Straight and narrow," as from *Pilgrim's Progress*
Onamatopoeia—He "slurped" down the drink.

Personification—The moon looked down through a clear bit of sky.
Metaphor—You are a clumsy ox.
Simile—His face turned as red as a beet.
Metonomy—The pen is mightier than the sword.
Allusion—She's a modern Florence Nightingale.

Figures of contrast and satire
Antithesis—Neighbors from far and near gathered for the reunion.
Epigram—An apple a day will keep the doctor away.
Irony—That's a fine way to act in front of company.
Apostrophe—Arise dead sons of the land and sweep the enemy from the shores.

Other
Hyperbole—I was tickled to death.
Euphemism—He is a sanitation engineer.
Synecdoche—He sold a hundred head of cattle.

10.21 Slanguage (Intermediate)

Objective: To increase student understanding of slang expressions.

Materials: Duplicating master, typewriter or pen.

Worksheet: Slanguage

1. Jack was playing some "canned music."
2. The ball missed hitting Jane by "the skin of her teeth."
3. He "stepped on the gas" when he noticed the time.
4. The old hound dog "kicked the bucket."
5. Bill's grades in mathematics were "nothing to write home about."
6. Mr. Thompson has a large "bread basket."
7. The car is in "A-1" condition.
8. "Balderdash!" exclaimed Susan.
9. Tim was acting like a "big cheese."
10. Mary thought the new dance was the "cat's pajamas."

Directions: Prepare a list of statements containing slang, such as the one on the worksheet. Duplicate the list and hand it to the class members.

Divide the class into several small groups. Tell them to decide on the literal meaning of each statement. When the teacher calls time, the students should share their explanations.

Variation: This activity could be modified to emphasize special slang used by different groups.

10.22 What's the Special Field? (Primary)

Objective: To increase student awareness of technical language associated with a field of study.

Materials: Unlined 3" × 5" index cards, felt-tip pen, and list of terms associated with particular field of study.

plus	inch	cent
add	divide	set
square	subtract	less than
equals	multiply	greater than

Directions: On each of the index cards, write words that are associated with a particular field of study, such as mathematics. Divide the class into several small groups. Give each group a set of cards. Tell them to decide on the meaning of the words and then to illustrate each with a drawing or example. For example, *plus* +. Each group should try to illustrate all of the words, When the teacher calls time, the students should share their illustrations and explain each one.

10.23 Fact or Opinion? (Intermediate)

Objective: To provide practice in differentiating fact from opinion.

Materials: Worksheet on which are listed sentences, some of which are of a factual nature and some of which are opinions.

Worksheet: Fact or Opinion?

Circle the numbers of the opinion sentences.

1. Joe seems very industrious to me.
2. Time passes slowly when you have nothing to do.
3. Bill has brown hair.
4. Florida's weather is more enjoyable than New York's.

---

5. Hawaii is the last state admitted to the United States.
6. Playing tennis is more fun than swimming.
7. Mary is over five feet tall.
8. Sarah is very short.
9. It isn't fair to take the parking area for another building.
10. Students should spend more time studying mathematics.
11. The book has 250 pages.

Directions: Instruct the students to circle the numbers of the items that are opinions. Discuss the answers after the students have completed the activity.

Variation: An activity could be developed to provide practice with common propaganda statements or other aspects of affective language.

11 Appreciation and Uses of Language

Students will put forth more effort in acquiring language skills and improving language abilities if their tasks are enjoyable and important to them. Perhaps one of the greatest weaknesses in the teaching of language arts is the failure to cultivate an appreciation of language through interesting and meaningful instructional activities.

This chapter focuses upon aspects of language which may be used to develop an appreciation of language and to create better attitudes and feelings toward language arts in the classroom. The first aspect involves literature, both prose and poetry; the second involves recreational activities which emphasize the enjoyment of language; the third aspect includes informational or real-life need situations, which may also be described as language survival skills in today's world.

The value of literature in producing an appreciation of language cannot be too strongly emphasized. However, literature may not necessarily be enjoyed by all students. The teacher must select and adapt literature-related activities carefully and sensitively in order to expand the literary interests of the students. Literature provides an opportunity for reading, for listening, for acting out; it provides characters to identify with and feel for, adventures to experience, places to go, and people to see; and literature can stimulate thought, imagination, and creativity. Activities included in the first section focus upon structured and syllabic poems, choral reading, and ways to respond to literature.

Language can also be fun, and teachers, observing the recreational games that children often play, have noted that many of them are language-based games. The insightful teacher will capitalize on such games and activities and use them to stimulate the language skills of the students. The teacher can also point out that the very games which are so enjoyable are also a part of language. The activities presented in the second section include some game-like usages of language which students will enjoy playing; at the same time, they would be manipulating language in such a way as to stimulate many of their language skills and thought processes.

Some students feel that language arts instruction "isn't really good for anything." Activities thus are needed which will be useful in immediate and obvious ways. With the ever-increasing complexity of twentieth-century society, it is becoming more and more important that certain language skills be taught as "survival skills." As students see from their own experiences how these skills can help them, they will be more eager to acquire the skills and participate whole-heartedly in activities involving such skills. In the end, the positive results may transfer to more standard language arts activities, with students realizing that improving all of their language skills can be beneficial to them. The activities included in this third section involve some of the survival skills which the students may find helpful in everyday life. These activities involve listening, speaking, reading, and writing in practical ways which can increase students' appreciation of and skills with language.

PROSE AND POETRY

11.1 Shape Poetry (Primary or Intermediate)

Objective: To provide a relaxed and interesting activity in which students can have fun with poetry.

Materials: Large sheets of laminated construction paper with large familiar shapes drawn on it.

Directions: Students are asked to write a poem and arrange the words to represent the topic.

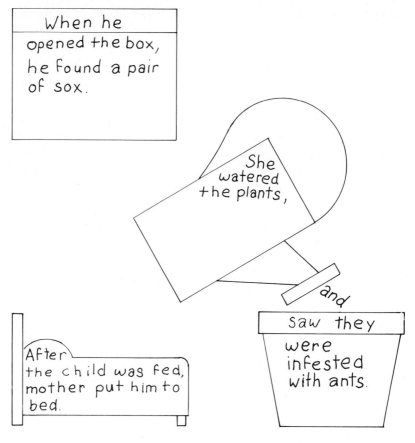

Variations:

1. When the students have completed their poems, the shapes can be cut out of construction paper and mounted to form an attractive and meaningful message.
2. Instead of writing verse in shapes, students can use one of the more standard verse forms, such as:

Haiku	5 syllable line	*Cinquain*	a noun
	7 syllable line		2 describing words
	5 syllable line		3 action words
			a statement or 4 more describing words
			a synonym for the original word
Lanterne	1 syllable line	*Tanka*	5 syllable line
	2 syllable line		7 syllable line
	3 syllable line		5 syllable line
	4 syllable line		7 syllable line
	1 syllable line		7 syllable line

Septolet   1 word
         2 words
         3 words
         4 words
         3 words
         2 words
         1 word

For this variation to be of most value, students need much exposure to published works utilizing these poetry forms, as well as a strong background in creative writing and poetry.

11.2 Alphabet Limericks (Intermediate)

Objective: To familiarize students with limerick forms.

Materials: Writing materials, rhyming dictionary, and teacher-supplied examples.

D

There once was a handsome young la*d*
Whose actions were less good than ba*d*
His friends came to abhor him,
Then they totally ignored him,
And now that bad lad is quite sa*d*!

Directions: Assign a letter of the alphabet. Students take this letter and create a limerick so that the final words of lines 1, 2, and 5 end with a word that has that letter in the final position. (Note: a limerick is a verse form with 5 lines; lines 1, 2, and 5 rhyme and have three metrical beats; lines 3 and 4 rhyme and have two metrical beats.)

Variation: The letter may be altered to an end *sound*; for example, instead of *v*, the sound *-ove*, represented by *shove* or *dove*, could be used. Here are some books of limericks:

Ehlert, Lois. *Limericks by Lear*. Cleveland: the World Publishing Co., 1965.

Rhys, Ernest. *A Book of Nonsense*. London: J. M. Dent and Sons, 1974.

Untermeyer, Louis. *The Golden Book of Fun and Nonsense.* New York: Western Publishing, 1972.

11.3 Choraling, Drama Style (Primary or Intermediate)

Objective: To provide students with experience in choral drama.

Materials: Various short stories, fables, fairy tales, or novels.

Directions: Select a familiar story which has a central group of characters in it, such as *The Three Little Pigs* or *Snow White and the Seven Dwarfs.* A group of students is designated as the character group. These students then go through the story together and find, first, all of the lines which are spoken by the character group together and then all of the incidents where the group acts or does the same thing. The students thoroughly familiarize themselves with the spoken parts and acting parts which are to be performed as a group. The teacher or another student reads aloud the story, and the group of characters responds in turn by speaking the parts in the correct place and by acting out the correct motions in the story.

Variation: Historical events can be written out for choral drama to form an ideal medium for this art.

11.4 Follow Along and Pantomime (Intermediate)

Objective: To enrich students' appreciation and understanding of literature through pantomime.

Materials: A novel, tale, short story, or scripted play, either in book or recorded version. Costumes as needed to identify the story's characters.

Directions: As the teacher reads aloud or plays the recorded version of a story, students who have been designated as the characters pantomime the parts. Those who have not been selected to pantomime the parts should provide the narration. Others may be responsible for staging or background sounds.

11.5 Now, "Play" It (Intermediate)

Objective: To increase students' understanding of drama by constructing a play from a fable, fairy tale, or novel.

Materials: Short stories, fables, fairy tales, and novels, writing materials.

Directions: The students read a short story, novel, fable, or fairy tale. Students are then asked to rewrite the story in play form, including the directions, staging cues, and the organization. Students then select the characters to act it out and direct the play, including costuming, staging, background music, sound effects, and props. Since this activity involves considerable technical knowledge, the teacher should precede the activity with explanations and in assisting students with such items as breaking the story into acts, converting narration to speech and/or action, and the like.

11.6 Role Playing (Primary or Intermediate)

Objective: To enrich students' understanding of literature by increasing their sympathetic understanding of the characters in a play.

Materials: Copies of a play, enough for each student.

Directions: First, have the students read the play silently. Then assign a character in the play to each student in the class; there may be two or three students assigned to each part. Ask them to study their assigned parts, thinking about the types of persons that their characters are. Begin the first oral reading of the play. Urge each student to read the dialogue in character. After the first reading, recast the play and have it read orally again. Continue until all have had an opportunity to participate. After each reading of the play, discuss techniques that could have improved each performance.

Variation:
1. Here are a number of valuable resources for play reading. *Aesop in the Afternoon.* Albert Cullum. Citation Press, 50 West 44th Street, New York 10036.

Favorite Plays for Classroom Reading. Donald D. Durrell and B. Alice Crossley. Plays, Inc., 8 Arlington Street, Boston, MA 02116.

Plays for Echo Reading. Donald D. Durrell and L. De Milia. Harcourt Brace Jovanovich, New York 10017.

Plays: The Drama Magazine for Young People. 8 Arlington Street, Boston, MA 02116.

Primary Plays for Reading. Ann R. Talbot. Curriculum Associates, 6 Henshaw Street, Woburn, MA 01801.

Scope Play Series. Scholastic Book Services, 50 West 44th Street, New York 10036.

Story Plays: Self-Directing Materials for Oral Reading. Margaret Rector and Douglas Rector. Harcourt Brace Jovanovich, 757 Third Avenue, New York 10017.

The Tiger's Bones and Other Plays for Children. Viking Press, 757 Third Avenue, New York 10017.

Thirty Plays for Classroom Reading. Donald D. Durrell and B. Alice Crossley. Plays Inc., 8 Arlington Street, Boston, MA 02116.

Walker Plays for Oral Reading. Henry Gilfond. Curriculum Associates, 6 Henshaw Street, Woburn, MA 01801

2. To enrich students' interpretation of poetry, choral reading of poetry is recommended. Materials needed include copies of a poem suitable in difficulty. Read the poem to the students or play a recording of a good speaker reading the poem. Discuss the poem with the students. Then read it or play the record several more times. Decide with the students the best combination of choral reading arrangement for the poem: unison, refrain, dialogue, line-a-child, or line-a-choir. Assign parts to the class members and let the students read their parts, using appropriate oral expression. Allow the students to evaluate their own efforts and to work on polishing the performance. See Activity 6.10.

11.7   Literature Contract (Intermediate)

Objective: To utilize a teacher-student constructed contract to help motivate reading.

Materials: Contract card.

Reading Contract

A. Read one of the following:

   1. Ogden Nash, "Adventures of Isabel"
   2. Shel Siverstein, "Sara Cynthia Sylvia Stout"
   3. Kaye Starbird, "Eat-It-All Elaine"
   4. A.A. Milne, "The King's Breakfast"
   5. Ogden Nash, "The Tale of Custard the Dragon"

B. Share your reactions one of these ways:

   1. Write a paragraph describing a character.
   2. Draw an incident in the poem.
   3. Write a humorous narrative story or poem.
   4. Make up a character and write a humorous incident about
      the character.
   5. Make a drawing of the character.

Choose one poem from A and one method from B for your contract.
I plan to do A _____ and B _____. I will have this contract completed by _____.

Student's signature _____

Teacher's signature _____

Directions: Students and teacher should cooperatively prepare
contract cards calling for a variety of assignments and tasks.
Guided by the teacher, students should select those most appropriate to their interests and needs. Contract cards should be used
to give students both a sense of control over their own reading
material (and thereby increasing interest in reading) and a sense
that they are learning necessary content.

RECREATIONAL

11.8 Shuffle a Word (Primary)

Objective: To provide a spelling activity in a recreational setting.

Materials: Writing materials, envelopes, and letters of the alphabet cut out of construction paper.

Directions: The students are shown a word with which they are familiar. Letters which are in the given word have been cut out of construction paper and put in an envelope. The students then rearrange the letters to spell words. The task is for them to see how many words they can spell using only the letters of the given word. After a word is discovered, it is written down. Students can compete against each other to see who can find the most words. One point is scored for each word correctly spelled; words incorrectly spelled take off one point. The winner is the student or team with the most points at the end of a specified time limit. A dictionary should be readily available for this game for students to check their words.

11.9   Mirror Words (Intermediate)

Objective: To introduce the concept of palindromes and to encourage word play.

Materials: Dictionary and writing materials.

Directions: Students search for palindromes, words or phrases which are spelled the same forwards and backwards: *mom, tot, refer*. Students may race over a period of twenty minutes to see who compiles the most words.

Variation: Older students can do the same activity using only words with more than three letters.

11.10   Change a Letter (Intermediate)

Objective: To provide a recreational spelling activity.

Materials: Laminated construction paper cards and felt tip markers.

```
┌─────────────────────┐
│     ┌──────┐        │
│     │ PALE │        │
│     └──────┘        │
│      SALE           │
│                     │
│      SANE           │
│                     │
│      SAND           │
│     ┌──────┐        │
│     │ SEND │        │
│     └──────┘        │
└─────────────────────┘
```

Directions: Students receive a laminated sheet that has a word printed at the top and a slightly different one at the bottom of the page (see example). By changing one letter at a time, new words are formed in successive steps. Each step must be a word. The objective is to reach the end word.

Variations:
1. This activity may be played as a race to see which of a group or team of students can reach the end word first with correctly spelled words.
2. Older students can use words with five or more letters.
3. The number of steps to be taken to arrive at the bottom word may be specified by the teacher.

11.11 ICU (Intermediate)

Objectives: To encourage word play and increase familiarity with words through phonic associations.

Materials: Writing materials and chalkboard examples.

I c u; do u c me, 2? (I see you; do you see me, too?)
D c s 2 cold 2day. (The sea is too cold today.)

Directions: Students are instructed to write as many sentences as possible using only letters of the alphabet or numerals to represent the words. Exact phonic duplications are not necessary: *D* can stand for "the," *S* can stand for "is," etc.

Variations:

1. This game may be played by older students competitively, lettering each sentence count as five points, and each letter-word in the sentence count as two additional points. The winner is the student (or team) with the most points at the end of an alloted time period.
2. One book that explores this idea is *CDB* by William Steig, (New York: E.P. Dutton, 1973).

11.12 Anagram-mar! (Primary or Intermediate)

Objective: To introduce the concept of anagrams and provide a recreational spelling activity.

Materials: List of words to be rearranged and writing materials.

Directions: The student is given a word and asked to write as many different words as possible, using all the letters from the original word. Some easy words are: *tool, ape, star, pal, rat.*

Variations:

1. Students may make up words which can be rearranged to form additional words, which can then be used by other students.
2. For more advanced students words of five or more letters may be used.

11.13 Unscramble the Words (Intermediate)

Objective: To encourage students to use orthographic generations.

Materials: Lists of words pertaining to a given subject which have all been respelled to form nonsense words.

Breakfast Foods

gseg	cnaob	sotta	iuejc
leettome	aagsues	kiml	lracee

Directions: Students are given lists of scrambled words, along with the topic to which all of the words pertain. In a given amount of time the students try to unscramble as many of the words as possible. The winner is the first person or team to unscramble all of the words; or, the winner is the team that has the most words unscrambled at the end of an alloted time period.

Variations:

1. Students may scramble as many words as they can in a ten minute period of time. They then exchange with their partner. The first one of the pair to unscramble their opponent's words wins. The answers are kept by each player for checking purposes.
2. For more difficult competition, the topic need not be told to the students, but they must guess it, after they have unscrambled all the words.

11.14 I'm Thinking of a Word (Intermediate)

Objective: To aid students' spelling and vocabulary skills by increasing their familiarity with and awareness of certain characteristics of words.

Materials: Lists of words to be used (such as spelling words).

Directions: One student is selected for the Word-Thinker, who selects a word. Four clues are available to the other students.

1. A *letter combination* in the word, such as "this word has an *l* and a *k*."
2. A *syllable* clue: "this word has one syllable."
3. A *sound* clue: "this word has a short *i* sound in it."
4. A *part of speech* clue: "this word can be used as a noun and a verb."

The students ask the Word-Thinker for one clue at a time. The first person to guess the word becomes the new Word-Thinker. If the word has not been guessed after four clues, the clues may be asked for again. If this happens, then the Word-Thinker gets to choose another word after the one selected has been guessed.

Variation: The entire dictionary may be used, but a total of sixteen word clues may be asked for: eight from the selected clue categories listed and eight "free" questions, such as "Does this word start with *a, b, c, d,* or *e*?" or "What is a synonym for this word?"

11.15 Word Chain (Intermediate)

Objective: To familiarize students with possible letter combinations which are constant from word to word.

Materials: Strips of paper marked into small divisions, cellophane tape, and felt-tip markers.

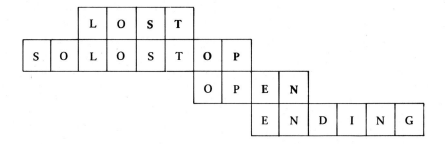

Directions: On the strips of paper, students write words that have at least two of the same letters in them. The words are then taped together as shown. The word chain is completed when the ending word can be taped to the beginning word or when no other words can be added. Chain may also go backwards from the beginning word.

REAL LIFE

11.16 Introduce Us (Primary)

Objective: To familiarize students with the social skills necessary for courteous introductions.

Materials: Cards with various names printed on them and a chart of characters to be introduced.

```
Let Me Introduce You to . . .

Miss Frog and Mr. Squirrel
Darth Vader and the Elf King
Dorothy and the Wizard of Oz
Charlotte and Wilbur
Aslan and the White Witch
Ben Franklin and Thomas Jefferson
King Arthur and Sir Lancelot
Moses and Pharaoh
Apple and Pear
Snow White and Cinderella
```

Directions: After explaining the proper forms of introduction, instruct two students to select from a stack of cards a character to portray; a third student is to be the *Introducer.* There is one card for each student in the class (or the number of participants). Students then find the person to whom they are to be introduced according to the chart. Introductions should include some sharing of information about both characters and something they have in common. Then another trio of students starts the next round. Play continues until all students or participants have had an opportunity to make an introduction.

11.17 Give Us a Call (Intermediate)

Objective: To facilitate the acquiring of courteous, functional telephone skills.

Materials: A pair of telephones and Sender Cards describing an incident or message and identifying a Receiver; cards are to be placed in envelopes.

```
Sender:   You have had an automobile accident and must report it;
          it involves injury.
Receiver: A police officer.
```

```
Sender:   You need to find out the homework assignment.
Receiver: A classmate
```

> Sender: You are a businessman or businesswoman wishing to leave an important message.
> Receiver: Secretary

> Sender: You are lost and need help, you call your parents.
> Receiver: Parents

> Sender: You are telling your grandparents that you will be flying in to see them.
> Receiver: Grandparent

> Sender: You are an actor booking some touring performances by phone.
> Receiver: Theater manager

> Sender: You are a camper placing an order for several items of camping gear.
> Receiver: Clerk in a clothing store—sender has the wrong number.

Directions: Students are divided into groups of two, and each group is given an envelope. One student is assigned the role of Sender; the other the role of Receiver. Telephone conversations are carried out according to the situation on the card.

11.18 Tell Me, Please (Primary or Intermediate)

Objective: To provide practice to ask for, give, and remember information efficiently.

Materials: Index cards and a list of various situations where information is needed. On each card, write one of the situations.

> Information, Please!
>
> 1. How to get to the nearest veterinary hospital as quickly as possible.
> 2 Where oysters, pimentos, napkins, and sour cream are in a grocery store.
> 3. How to put together the bicycle you got for your birthday.
> 4. Where the Samoan Islands are in relation to Australia.

5. How to find library books on guinea pigs.
6. How to tell if you're being conned into something.
7. How to tell a real friend from a fake one.
8. Where the northern elf kingdom disappeared to so suddenly.
9. How to make punch for your mother's surprise birthday party.
10. How to build a doghouse for the puppy you found.
11. How to tell the difference between poisonous and edible mushrooms.
12. What to do in case of emergency with the children you're babysitting.
13. What to do if someone gets sick while they're with you.
14. What to do if you're cornered by some older guys.

Directions: Students are paired into groups. One student in each pair receives an index card which describes a situation requiring the giving and receiving of information. The student who has the index card then asks the other student for the information which is needed. (The second student does not know what is to be asked until the question is posed. From there an explanation develops.) At the end of the explanation, both students write what information was given to make sure everything was remembered. Comparisons of answers are then made and any corrections or additions which must be added are also made.

11.19 Make Your Own Phone Book (Primary)

Objective: To provide familiarity with the telephone book.

Materials: A telephone book, notebooks, paper, writing and drawing materials, index dividers, scissors, tape, and example themes.

Help Emergency numbers: police, ambulance, fire department, doctor, close neighbor, drug assistance, or suicide assistance organization

Friends

Important Numbers drug store, doctor, time and temperature, grocery store, veterinarian, parents' place of occupation, school number, recreational building, day care center

Important People school teacher, landlord, grandparents, home phone

Fun Places movies, toy store, pet store, zoo, amusement park, fair, book store, sports store, swimming or recreational park

Directions: Students and teacher discuss the purpose and content of the telephone book. Students then divide their notebooks with the index dividers, according to the categories chosen; they then construct their own telephone books, using available telephone books as references. The students then discuss and decide on the best place to keep their own phone notebooks at all times. The telephone notebooks can also be decorated and be made attractive.

11.20 Planning Ahead (Intermediate)

Objective: To facilitate the ability to make plans.

Materials: Writing materials, a variety of information resources, and sample topics.

1. Plan a weekend camping trip for the entire class.
2. Plan a slumber party or birthday party.
3. Plan a soccer match between your class and the class across the hall.
4. Plan a field trip to the zoo, the caverns, the bakery, or other place to visit.
5. There has been some theft in your classroom neighborhood.
6. Your class wants to clean up an eye-sore across the street.
7. A highway is to be built through the forest that you and your friends play in. Plan your course of action to try to prevent.
8. Plan a cookout for your class.
9. Plan an awards assembly for the end of the year.
10. Plan an all-school field day.
11. Plan a school dance or fund-raising project.
12. Plan a trip and program for a nursing home at Thanksgiving.
13. Plan a spring musical program, play, or talent show.
14. Plan an entire puppet show from beginning to end.

Directions: Students are assigned by small groups (three to five) to a topic which they are to plan. Topics should be discussed and *all* the details involved should be worked out. After all the planning has been completed, a report is written, telling:

What is needed	Where it will take place
What is to be done	Transportation
Who will be involved	Expense
When it will start and end	Who will be in charge of what items

The topic could be one which will be implemented. If this is possible, then the entire class can be assigned to several small groups which are all discussing the same topic.

Variation: Plans of this nature may be made by individual students and serve entirely as a writing activity.

11.21 Gripe, Gripe! (Intermediate)

Objective: To teach students how to make courteous but effective complaints.

Materials: Laminated construction paper and a list of complaint items.

I'd Like to Complain!

1. You are sold a pet mynah bird that won't talk.
2. You are returning a shirt with olive, purple, pink, and rust brown polka dots to a store for a refund.
3. You feel like you are being given too much work and not enough in wages.
4. The school building is so cold your fingers are stiff.
5. You received the wrong record in the mail from your record club.
6. A fall jacket you ordered in October has not yet come, and it is already March.
7. You are being ridiculed by some of your classmates.
8. You asked for a hamburger and they gave you liver and onions.
9. You and several other customers were treated discourteously at a department store.
10. You were shortchanged a dollar by a store cashier.
11. You paid for an ice cream cone thirty minutes ago but the waitress has apparently forgotten you.

Directions: Students are grouped into pairs; one student receives a sheet which has printed on it a problem about which a complaint is to be made. The student with the problem then lists on the laminated sheet all the points which must be presented in the complaint. The complaint is then presented to the second student who is directed to try to counter every possible argument. The discussion is completed when an agreement is reached.

Variation: These complaints may also be expressed in a letter.

11.22 Let Me Tell You (Intermediate)

Objective: To encourage students to give information to others in a complete, concise manner.

Materials: Writing materials, poster board, and information cards.

Make a poster to put in the local grocery store and bank to advertise your upcoming class talent show for raising money.

Make up an announcement to go on the radio and over your school's public address system announcing the track and field competition between the school track team and the local policemen's organization.

You have been asked to review a television program from the viewpoint of your class. Select a television show and interview your classmates. Put the information into review form.

Write and act out the script for a television commercial to tell about your school band and choir spring festival.

Directions: Students are given a situation which requires giving out information. They then fulfill the task and distribute or display the results.

11.23 Explain Yourself (Primary or Intermediate)

Objective: To provide students with opportunities to give an explanation, either orally or written, of problems, dilemmas, circumstances, or reasons for behavior.

Materials: File of problem cards.

You have been accused of hitting the new student whose nose is bleeding badly. You didn't even touch the new student, however.

You must explain that you were late for school today because you stopped and tried to find the owner of a puppy that was following you.

A group of your classmates come in the room during recess and find some of their belongings missing. You are the only one in the room when they come in.

Directions: Students are divided into small groups of four to six students. One student is selected as the defendant; the remaining students serve as a jury. The student presents the problem given on the file card. An explanation of the situation, justification of actions, or proposed solution is presented to the jury. The jury members can ask questions of the defendant, trying to cause an error. The defendant answers the questions accordingly. After the questioning has been completed, the jury votes as to whether or not to believe the case presented by the defendant.

Variations:

1. The explanations may be written down in essay form for the jury to read and decide on.
2. Do not overlook classroom situations that arise which call for explanation.

12 Language Arts Within the Content Areas

Listening, speaking, and writing are integral parts of the major content areas of the elementary school curriculum: literature, social studies, science and health, and mathematics. A vital language arts program thus contributes to those areas by improving the requisite skills. Moreover language arts activities can be integrated into the basic instructional program and invigorate the entire curriculum. The activities in this chapter have been designed, on the one hand, to increase the relevant skills in the various content areas; additionally, they should be effectively inserted into the ongoing programs of any of the other content areas.

SOCIAL STUDIES

12.1 Unit Words (Primary)

Objective: To improve spelling skills related to a unit of social studies—transportation in this example.

Materials: A file of scrambled words dealing with transportation.

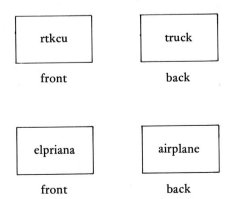

rtkcu
front

truck
back

elpriana
front

airplane
back

Directions: As unit of transportation is underway, arouse students' interest in transportation words. Put file out for team quizzing, partner work, or free-time activity. When students can success-fully unscramble all the words, a certificate of achievement can be given. The certificate could be related to transportation.

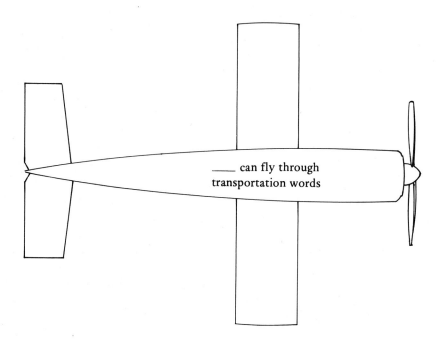

_____ can fly through
transportation words

Variation: Other unit-word activities can be developed for any of the other content areas.

12.2 Social Studies Word Search Puzzle (Primary or Intermediate)

Objective: To develop vocabulary related to social studies.

Materials: Duplicating master; typewriter and/or pen; word search puzzle (words chosen from social studies textbooks).

Directions: Distribute copies of the puzzle. Instruct students to locate and circle words related to social studies. Tell them that the words may be horizontal, vertical, or diagonal, and either forward or backward. The puzzle may appear without a list of definitions or words.

Variation: Word search puzzles can be developed for terms in any of the other content areas.

Social Studies Word Search Puzzle

P	N	A	L	U	S	N	I	N	E	P
Y	R	T	N	U	O	C	S	T	D	L
N	S	L	E	A	S	K	T	N	N	A
I	E	E	P	N	H	O	H	E	A	I
A	A	D	P	F	O	G	M	N	L	N
R	B	S	E	I	R	Z	U	I	N	Z
R	O	O	T	E	E	F	S	T	I	E
E	A	I	S	L	A	N	D	N	A	R
T	R	L	O	D	I	L	D	O	M	C
L	D	E	S	E	R	T	A	C	T	Z

Starter definitions
One of the principal land masses of the earth (continent)
A barren region, usually caused by low rainfall (desert)
A land mass surrounded by water (island)
A long projection of land into water (peninsula)

Starter words

acres	lido	seaboard
country	mainland	shore
field	plain	soil

12.3 What's in the News? (Intermediate)

Objective: To provide practice in locating information in the newspaper.

Materials: Copies of newspapers, appropriate for reading level; sets of questions, as suggested below.

Worksheet: What's in the News?

Directions: Use your newspaper to answer these questions.

1. On what page can you find sports?
2. What movie would you choose to attend?
3. What is your favorite comic character in this paper?
4. On what page can you find listings about things to buy?
5. Which restaurant would you select? Why?
6. What is your horoscope?
7. On what page are the editorials?
8. What TV programs would you like to watch tonight?

Directions: Procedures are given on the worksheet. Answers may be oral or written.

12.4 Composing on Social Studies Topics (Intermediate)

Objective: To utilize the composing of poetry to increase interest in social studies.

Materials: Sample cinquains, as follows:

Lincoln
Sixteenth president
Thinking, speaking, serving
Equal rights for all
Honest

Shiloh
Tennessee battleground
Fighting, shooting, killing
Thousands of wasted lives
Bloody

Directions: Present the sample cinquains. Explain the features: first line: one word giving the title; second line: two words describing the topic; third line: three words expressing an action; fourth line: four words expressing a feeling; fifth line: another word for the title. Encourage efforts at writing such a patterned poem on a social studies topic.

Variations:

1. A similar activity could involve a topic from any of the content areas.
2. A similar activity could involve the writing of other poetry patterns, such as couplets; triplets; quatrains; limericks; haiku; lanterne; septolet; tanka; or free verse; see Activity 11.1 for other forms.

12.5 Yesterday's News Today (Intermediate)

Objective: To utilize functional writing on an historical topic.

Materials: Model of a newspaper article.

Stop the Presses!

Early yesterday morning, 189 Japanese planes bombed the American naval base at Pearl Harbor, Hawaii during a surprise attack. Around 170 U.S. planes were destroyed on the ground before they could be manned for battle. There were 18 ships sunk or badly damaged and about 3,700 American casualties, including 2,400 dead.

Later in the day, President Franklin D. Roosevelt condemned the act and said that it was "a day that will live in infamy." The United States will officially declare war on Monday, December 8.

Directions: Explain that the idea is to take a topic from the past and prepare a newspaper article as though the event had just occurred. Point out that a good guide to writing a news account is to answer the questions: *Who* is the story about? *What* has happened? *When* did the event occur? *Where* does the action take place? *Why* did it happen? and *How* did it happen?

SCIENCE/HEALTH

12.6 Science Concentration (Intermediate)

Objective: To increase familiarity with content terms—science terms, here.

Materials: A 3' X 4' board, cardboard or poster board, on which are attached twenty-four numbered pockets.

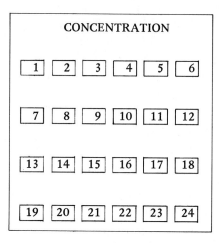

Directions: A word is written on each of the first twelve cards; their definitions are written on the last twelve. Cards are placed face down in the pockets. This game is to be played with two students or two teams. One at a time, the students choose two numbers. The cards are turned over. If the word matched the definition, one point is scored. The two cards are removed from the board. If the cards do not match, they are put back in the same pockets from which they came. Play continues until all words and definitions have been matched.

Variation: This game can be developed for terms of any of the other content areas.

12.7 Science/Health Word Search Puzzle
(Primary or Intermediate)

Objective: To develop content area vocabulary.

Materials: Duplicating master; typewriter and/or pen; puzzle similar to the one below. Choose words from the students' textbooks.

Science/Health Word Search Puzzle

S	A	T	R	O	A	P	G	N	U	L
L	Y	M	P	H	B	L	O	O	D	N
L	L	T	O	H	E	A	L	T	H	O
E	I	Y	R	E	L	S	P	E	C	D
C	V	E	G	A	B	M	U	L	A	N
S	E	N	L	R	P	A	L	E	M	E
K	R	D	A	T	O	E	S	K	O	T
I	J	I	N	E	R	V	E	S	T	R
N	N	K	D	N	E	E	L	P	S	C

Starter definitions

The large artery that carries blood from the heart to branch arteries (aorta)

A cell or group of cells that removes materials from the blood (gland)

A large glandular organ that secretes bile (liver)

The fluid part of blood (plasma)

The tough cord of tissue that unites a muscle with some other part of the body (tendon)

Starter words

amoeba	lung
blood	pulse
health	skeleton

Directions: Distribute copies of the puzzle. Instruct students to locate words related to the content area and then to circle the words. Tell students the words may appear in any order on the puzzle—horizontal, vertical, diagonal, forward, or backward.

Variation: Word search puzzles may be developed for terms of any of the other content areas.

12.8 Build a Word (Intermediate)

Objective: To increase familiarity with common prefixes, suffixes, and root words found in content area vocabulary—here, in science/health materials.

Materials: Duplicating master; typewriter and/or pen; lists of word parts (choose the prefixes, suffixes, and roots from terms in the students' textbooks).

Prefix	Root	Suffix
an-	anthropo	-itis
anti-	bio	-logy
micro-	geo	-meter

Directions: Distribute the list of word parts. Instruct the students to form as many words as they can using each word part. Have them define each word they form. They are given a point for each correctly defined word. A time limit may be placed on this activity. The students may be allowed to use the dictionary or their science textbooks.

Variation: This activity can be developed for terms in any of the other content areas.

12.9 Words from Science (Primary or Intermediate)

Objective: To provide opportunity for building word lists that are related to a content topic—science terms here.

Materials: Science textbooks, pencil and paper, and examples of topics and words.

Moon	Matter	Human body
craters	compound	blood
earth	elements	bone
orbit	gas	cell
reflect	liquid	epithelia
rotate	mixture	ligament
satellite	molecule	muscle
space	oxygen	nerve
stars	properties	respiratory
sun	solid	skeleton
telescope	volume	tissue

Directions: Instruct the students, after a unit of work, to use their science textbook to locate words associated with a particular topic. The teacher may propose the topics, or the students may be permitted to decide upon the topics. The meaning of the words may be discussed; some may be illustrated through drawings or diagrams; and perhaps a vocabulary notebook may be gradually developed over a period of time. Of course, a science dictionary may be an outcome of such activities.

Variation: A good activity could evolve by putting the words on individual cards, mixing them, and having teams race against one another in placing them under the topic with which it is related.

MATHEMATICS

12.10 Specialized Word Meaning (Intermediate)

Objective: To increase familiarity with words of multiple meanings found in the content areas, here in mathematics.

Materials: A dictionary for each student, chalkboard and chalk, list of mathematics terms that have multiple meanings (as *set, foot, line, product, ray*).

Directions: Write the terms on the board. Set a time limit for the exercise. Instruct students to compose sentences with the words listed, using the different meanings of the words in separate sentences. The student scores a point for each correct sentence that uses the different meanings of the word. Two points are scored for using the word with its correct mathematical meaning. The sentences cannot be simple definitions, such as "Set means . . ."

Variation: A similar activity can be developed for the multiple-meaning words commonly found in any of the other content area textbooks.

12.11 Math Symbol Language (Primary or Intermediate)

Objective: To increase recognition of the meanings of mathematical symbols and numerals.

Materials: Game board similar to the one shown, unlined index cards (on the index cards, write meanings of the symbols that appear on the board or other ways to express the symbols or numerals), tokens for players, felt-tip marker.

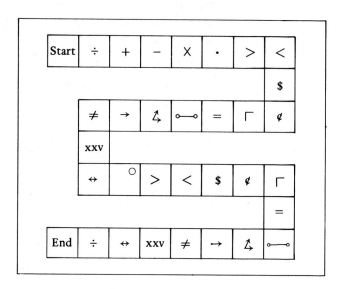

Terms

divide	add	subtract	multiply
greater than	less than	dollar	cent
equals	line segment	angle	ray
25	line	degree	divide

Directions: The index cards are shuffled and placed face down. The first player draws a card and advances to the nearest symbol of the card. If the player does not recognize the meaning, he or she cannot move; if the player moves to an incorrect space, he or she must lose two spaces. The first player to reach the end is the winner.

12.12 Mathematics Word Search Puzzle
(Primary or Intermediate)

Objective: To develop vocabulary related to content area—here, mathematics.

Materials: Duplicating master, typewriter and/or pen, puzzle similar to the one below. (Choose words from mathematics textbooks.)

Mathematics Word Search Puzzle

F	A	C	T	O	R	O	R	E	Z
R	U	B	P	R	I	M	E	S	D
A	F	N	E	V	E	I	C	L	I
C	W	D	C	R	N	P	A	R	G
T	H	D	H	T	J	N	R	E	I
I	O	A	E	O	I	K	D	B	T
O	L	G	D	D	I	O	I	M	O
N	E	D	R	L	M	T	N	U	T
R	P	O	S	U	L	P	A	N	A
M	U	S	Y	M	B	O	L	R	L

Clues

When you combine two addends, you _____. (add)

"There are twenty people in this room" is an example of the _____ use of number. (cardinal)

Seven is a one _____ number. (digit)

Four is an _____ number. (even)

Four is a _____ of both eight and twelve. (factor)

Terms

fraction	number	ratio
function	plus	whole
integer	prime	zero

Directions: Distribute copies of the puzzle. Instruct students to locate words related to mathematics and then to circle the words. Tell students that the words may appear in any order on the puzzle—horizontal, vertical, diagonal, backward, or forward.

Variation: Word search puzzles can be developed for terms of any of the other content areas.

12.13 Abbreviation Card Game (Intermediate)

Objective: To familiarize students with the meanings of the abbreviations commonly used in content area—here, mathematics materials.

Materials: Felt-tip pen, unlined index cards (on some of the index cards write mathematical abbreviations; on other cards, except one, write the corresponding meanings; on the last card write *No Match*).

Directions: The cards are shuffled and distributed to the players. The rules of the card game *Old Maid* are followed. "Books" consist of an abbreviation and its meaning. The *No Match* card is treated like the *Old Maid*. The player left with this card loses.

Variation: A similar activity can be developed using abbreviations of terms from any of the other content areas.

12.14 Listen and Do Mental Mathematics
(Primary or Intermediate)

Objective: To provide practice in listening to orally administered mathematics problems.

Materials: Sets of mathematics problems. These can be taken from mathematics textbooks.

Directions: The problems and exercises are read to the students. They are not to use pencil or paper in the computation.

LIBRARY SKILLS

12.15 Map the Library (Primary or Intermediate)

Objective: To increase familiarity with library resources.

Materials: Large sheet of drawing paper and a pencil, pen, or crayon.

Directions: Take the students on a tour of the school library. Point out the locations of important resources. Assist the students in drawing a map of the library which should include the card catalog, and the checkout desk, the location of different books, magazines, and newspapers, and other such features as the reference area, vertical file, carrels, tables, and the audiovisual equipment area.

12.16 Using Catalog Cards (Primary or Intermediate)

Objective: To increase familiarity with the library's filing system—author, title, subject.

Materials: Sample cards on bulletin board.

Author Card

```
j633.15
A544c
   Aliki
      Corn Is Maize, illus. by Aliki.
   NY: T.Y. Crowell, 1976
   illus.
```

Title Card

```
j633.15  Corn   Is   Maize,
            Aliki
```

Subject Card

```
   Corn
j633.15
   Aliki
      Corn Is Maize, illustrated by
   Aliki. NY: T.Y. Crowell,
   1976 illus.
```

Directions: After study of the cards, a series of questions (either on worksheet or orally) should be presented:

1. On the author card, where is the author's name placed?
2. What four pieces of information are given on the author card?
3. Where is the author's name on the title card?
4. Where is the book title on the subject card?

5. If you know the book's title but not its author, what card would you use?
6. What kind of card would you use to see if the library has a book on a particular subject?
7. What does the *j* mean on the cards?
8. What does the call number mean?
9. By what letter are each of the cards alphabetized in the card catalog?

Variation: Give each student a book and three index cards. Have each student use the model cards as guides and construct an author card, title card, and subject card for his or her book.

12.17 Dewey Decimal Flash Card Game (Intermediate)

Objective: To increase familiarity with the Dewey Decimal System.

Materials: Index cards (with titles on one side and classification names and numbers on the other) and a poster showing the major divisions of the Dewey Decimal System and related key numbers,

Dewey Decimal System	
000–099	General Works (bibliographies, encyclopedias, and other reference books)
100–199	Philosophy (psychology, ethics)
200–299	Religion (including mythology)
300–399	Social Sciences (law, government, education, vocations, civics, economics)
400–499	Language (including dictionaries)
500–599	Science (mathematics, physics, chemistry, biology, zoology, botany)
600–699	Applied Science and Useful Arts (medicine, engineering, agriculture, aviation)
700–799	Fine Arts and Recreation (painting, music, photography)
800–899	Literature (poetry, plays, novels)
900–000	History, Geography, Travel, Biography

Directions: Display and discuss the poster before the game is played. Provide preliminary activities such as taking a tour of the school or public library. Using the Dewey Decimal System as a guide, find books in different subject areas.

Prepare a stack of index cards with titles on one side and classification names and numbers on the other. Have pairs play the game: one student holds up a title and the partner gives the classification and number.

12.18 Encyclopedia Search (Intermediate)

Objective: To provide practice in choosing the correct volume of the encyclopedia.

Materials: Duplicating master, typewriter or pen, set of encyclopedias or a poster that shows the volumes of a set of encyclopedias, and a worksheet with questions such as the following:

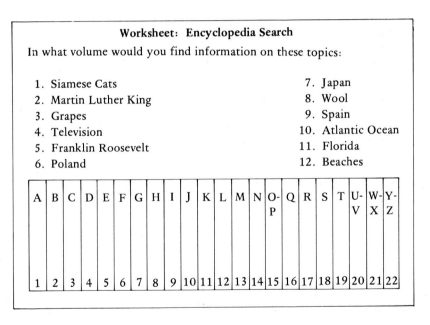

Worksheet: Encyclopedia Search

In what volume would you find information on these topics:

1. Siamese Cats
2. Martin Luther King
3. Grapes
4. Television
5. Franklin Roosevelt
6. Poland

7. Japan
8. Wool
9. Spain
10. Atlantic Ocean
11. Florida
12. Beaches

A	B	C	D	E	F	G	H	I	J	K	L	M	N	O-P	Q	R	S	T	U-V	W-X	Y-Z
1	2	3	4	5	6	7	8	9	10	11	12	13	14	15	16	17	18	19	20	21	22

Directions: Prepare worksheets and duplicate them. Distribute the worksheets and tell students to refer to the set of encyclopedias or the encyclopedia poster to decide which volume contains the information. Let the students check their own answers by referring to a set of encyclopedias. If a poster is used, prepare an answer key for them to refer to in checking their answers.

12.19 Atlas Questions (Intermediate)

Objective: To provide experience with the atlas.

Materials: Atlas and a set of questions.

1. How far is _____ from where we live?
2. What route would be taken to get to _____ by plane? Train? Car?
3. What kind of weather does _____ have?
4. What is the population of _____ ?
5. How many miles above sea level is _____ ?

Directions: Students can choose a city of interest and then go to the atlas to find answers to the set of questions.

12.20 What Are the Almanac Facts? (Intermediate)

Objective: To provide practice with the almanac.

Materials: Duplicating master, typewriter, or pen, almanacs, and a set of questions.

Only the Facts!

Directions: Using the information on the table of contents of the almanac, find the following:

1. Who were the twelfth president and vice-president of the United States? (Zachary Taylor, Millard Fillmore)
2. What is the world's tallest building at this time? Where is it located? How tall is it? (Sears Tower, USA, Chicago, Illinois. 1,454 ft. or 110 stories)
3. Where is the geographic center of the U.S. and what is its latitude and longitude? (West of Castle Rock, Butte County, South Dakota lat. N 44°58' long. W 103°46')
4. What is the equivalent measure in feet and meters of a fathom? (6 feet or 1.8288 meters)
5. What is the zip code of East Moline, Illinois? (61244)

---

6. Who was the 1930 Nobel Prize winner in medicine and for what achievement? (Karl Landsteiner; for discovery of human blood groups)
7. What was the Academy Award Winner for Best Picture of 1949? (*All the King's Men*)
8. Who was Miss America of 1951 and where is her home town? (Yolande Betbeze from Mobile, Alabama)
9. What disaster occurred on April 15, 1912, in the North Atlantic? (The *Titanic* struck an iceberg and sank, 1,500 dead)
10. What was the name of the Kentucky Derby winner of 1965 and the jockey who rode to victory? (Lucky Debonair, W. Shoemaker)

Directions: Prepare question sheets and duplicate them. Distribute the worksheets and instruct students to answer the questions. When the worksheets are completed, discuss the answers and the means of finding them with the class.

Variations:
1. Questions can be a part of a bulletin-board activity focusing upon the almanac.
2. A similar activity can be developed with other interesting "famous facts books" or "books of quotations."

12.21 Index Search (Intermediate)

Objective: To provide practice with using an index.

Materials: Sample index and a set of questions.

Index

Adjectives	Pronouns
in complete predicate, 30–34	definition, 21
in complete subject, 27–29	subject, 23–25
definition, 26	
in a series, 25	Verbs
	definition, 50
Adverbs	kinds
definition, 72	action, 56
suffix - *ly*, 74–76	linking, 58

Nouns	(Verbs)
common and proper, 8–12	subject-verb agreement, 60
definition, 7	tense
noun markers, 10–12	future, 63
possessive, 17–19	past, 63
proper, 10–12	present, 62
singular and plural, 13–15	

Directions: Ask the students to use the index to answer such questions as:

1. On what page would you find the definition of adjective?
2. On what page would you find "linking verbs" mentioned?
3. What pages contain information about noun markers?
4. Where would you look to find information about subject pronouns? What main heading did you look under to find it?
5. Is there information about action verbs on page 52?
6. What page discusses past tense of verbs? What subheading did you look under?
7. Find the meaning of "verb" and write it. Cite the page number.

Variations:
1. Similar activities can be developed for a want-ad index, daily paper index, and catalogue index.
2. Other parts of textbooks can receive similar attention: table of contents, appendices, bibliographies, and glossaries.

12.22 Interpreting a Flow Chart (Intermediate)

Objective: To provide practice with interpreting graphic aids often found in research references.

Materials: A sample flow chart.

Directions: Draw a flow chart such as the one in the illustration. Students volunteer to follow the directions on the chart. Each symbol is to be interpreted until the task is completed. The volunteer describes each decision (using a numerical example) to illustrate.

Variation: Other graphic aids commonly met in research references include maps, graphs, tables and illustrations. Similar activities can be developed for each type of graphic aid.

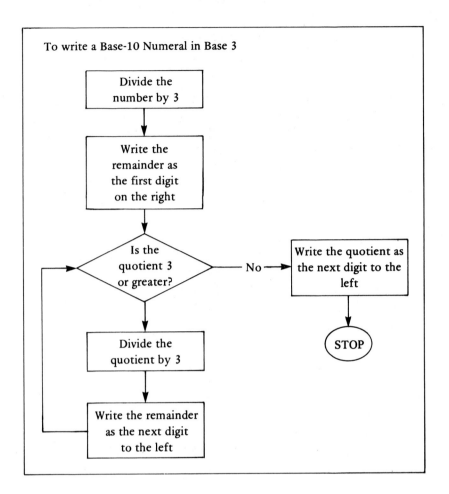

To write a Base-10 Numeral in Base 3

- Divide the number by 3
- Write the remainder as the first digit on the right
- Is the quotient 3 or greater? — No → Write the quotient as the next digit to the left → STOP
- Divide the quotient by 3
- Write the remainder as the next digit to the left

ORGANIZATIONAL SKILLS

12.23 Note-taking (Intermediate)

Objective: To increase note-taking skills.

Materials: Multiple copies of an informational article, preferably one related to topics currently being studied in the classroom.

Directions: Ask the students to read the article and take notes about it. When they finish, let them compare their notes with a teacher-prepared set of notes on the article. This activity should be preceded with a review of important points about taking notes, such as,

1. to cite bibliographical reference data
2. to make notes in the form of key words and phrases
3. to be careful to indicate notes that are direct quotations.

12.24 Outlining (Intermediate)

Objective: To provide practice in making outlines.

Materials: Multiple copies of an article currently being studied in a content area, duplicating master, typewriter or pen, and an incomplete outline of the article.

Classes of Vertebrates

    I.   There are many similarities among classes
       A.
       B.
       C.
       D.
   II.   There are many differences among classes
       A.
       B.
       C.
       D.

Directions: After discussing the purpose and the making of an outline, distribute copies of the article and the incomplete outlines. Instruct students to fill in the missing parts of the outline.

12.25 Summarizing (Intermediate)

Objective: To provide practice in writing summaries.

Materials: Duplicating master, typewriter or pen, a fairly long article dealing with a content area subject currently being studied by the students.

Directions: Distribute the article. Ask students to summarize each paragraph in one sentence. Discuss their summary sentences in class.

Appendix A

Multilevel Language Arts Instructional Materials

1. American Book Company, 135 W. 50 St., New York, NY 10020: *Our Language Today*—level 1-8; *Patterns of Language*—level 1-8.
2. American Guidance Service, Circle Pines, MN 55014: *Peabody Language Development Kits.*
3. Barnell Loft, Ltd., 958 Church St., Baldwin, NY 11510: *Capitalization and Punctuation*—set A-I, grades 1-9.
4. Benefic Press, 10300 W. Roosevelt Rd., Westchester, IL 60153: *Oral Reading and Linguistics*—grades 1-6.
5. BFA Educational Media, 3470 Old Fairburn Rd., Atlanta, GA 30331: *Tell the Whole Story Series*—super 8 silent filmloops, primary, elementary.
6. Bowmar Publishing Corp., 622 Rodier Dr., Glendale, CA 91201: *ABC Serendipity*—grades 2-6; *Language Stimulus Program*—grades 3-8.
7. Churchill Films, 662 N. Robertson Blvd., Los Angeles, CA 90069: *Let's Write a Story*—film.
8. Communicad, Box 541, Wilton, CT 06897: *Wordcraft*—vocabulary program, grades 4-6; remedially 7-13.
9. Coronet Instructional Media, 65 E. South Water St., Chicago, IL 60601: *How to Prepare a Class Report*—film; *Improve Your Handwriting*—film; *Improve Your Pronunciation*—film; *Improve Your Spelling*—film; *Know Your Library*—film; *Listen Well, Learn Well*—filmstrip.
10. Curriculum Associates, 94 Bridge St., Chapel Hill Park, Newton, MA 02518: *A Child-Centered Language Arts Program*—grades 3-8; *Children Writing Research Reports*—intermediate, middle school; *Elaborative Thinking Sets*—primary, intermediate; *Letters in Words*—preprimary, primary; *Right Is Write*—grades K-8; *Thirty Lessons in Outlining*—organization skills for elementary grades; *Word Growth Programs*—spelling, grades 2-6.
11. Disneyland Records, Walt Disney Educational Materials, Glendale, CA 91201: *The Art of Learning Through Movement*—grades K-6.
12. Doubleday Multimedia, Box 11607, 1371 Reynolds Ave., Santa Ana, CA 92705: *Learning Language Through Songs and Symbols*—sets I, II, and III, filmstrips, teaching guide; *More Road to Meaning*—filmstrips, teacher's guide, duplicator master.
13. Ealing Films, Chapel Bridge Park, Newton, MA 02158: *Springboards to Writing*—grades 4-6, film; *Story Starters*—grades 1-3, film.
14. Economy Company, Box 25308, 1901 N. Walnut, Oklahoma City, OK 73125: *Continuous Progress in Spelling.*

15. Educational Developmental Laboratories, Inc., 1221 Ave. of the Americas, New York, NY 10036: *EDL Study Skills Library*; *Listen-Think Tapes*.

16. Educational Progress, Box 45663, Tulsa, OK 74145: *Spelling Progress Laboratory*—grades 2-6.

17. Educational Services, Inc., Box 219, Stevensville, MI 49127: *Anchor*—intermediate language arts; *Flair*—suggestions for creative writing; *Spice*—games, ideas, activities for primary language arts.

18. Encyclopaedia Britannica Educational Corporation, 425 N. Michigan Ave., Chicago, IL 60611: *Language Experiences in Early Childhood*; *Language Experiences in Reading*—levels 1, 2, 3, and 4; *Magic Moments*—twenty 16mm sound films.

19. Follett Education Corporation, 1010 W. Washington Blvd., Chicago, IL 60607: *Follett Spelling Program*; *Spelling and Writing Patterns*—grades 1-8; *The World of Language*—grades 1-6.

20. Ginn and Company, 191 Spring St., Lexington, MA 02173: *Ginn Individualized Spelling Program*; *Invitations to Speaking and Writing Creatively*; *Let's Listen*.

21. Harcourt Brace Jovanovich, 757 Third Ave., New York, NY 10017: *The Bookmark Reading Program*, M. Early—grades K-8; *Durrell-Murphy Phonics Practice Program*; *Language for Daily Use*—eight levels; *The Palo Alto Reading Program*, Sequential Steps in Reading—grades K-3; *Plays for Echo Reading*—books and records, primary; *Sound and Sense in Spelling*—grades 1-8; *Speech-to-Print Phonics: A Phonics Foundation for Reading*; *The Story Plays: Self-directing Materials for Oral Reading*.

22. D.C. Heath and Co., 125 Spring St., Lexington, MA 02173: *Communicating*—The Heath English Series, levels 1-6; *English Is Our Language*—grades K-6; *On My Own in Spelling*—grades 3-6; *Reading Caravan*—grades 1-6.

23. Holt, Rinehart and Winston, Inc., 383 Madison Ave., New York, NY 10017: *Holt's Impact*—grades 7-9; *The Owl Program*; *Snoopy's Phonics Program*—grades K-6; *Sounds of Language Readers*—K-8; *Story Starter Film Loops*—grades 1-6; *Writing Center*—set of stimulus cards.

24. Houghton Mifflin Company, 1 Beacon St., Boston, MA 02107: *Interaction*—K-12; *Listen and Do*; *Listen and Learning*.

25. Ideal School Supply, 11000 S. Lavergne Ave., Oak Lawn, IL 60453: *Learn to Listen*—cassettes and lessons, primary.

26. Individualized Instruction Incorporated, Box 25308, Oklahoma City, OK 73125: *Continuous Spelling Kit*—intermediate; *Continuous Spelling Kit*—primary.

27. Instructional Fair, 4158 Lake Michigan Dr., Grand Rapids, MI 49504: *Creative Writing Masters*—grades 1-6.

28. The Instructo Corporation, Cedar Hollow and Matthews Rd., Paoli, PA 19301: *Contractions Magic Show*—grades 2-5; *Decoding Everyday Abbreviations*—grades 2-5; *Homonyms*—grades 2-5; *Learning When to Capitalize (and When NOT)*—grades 2-5; *Letter Writing*—series of 4 transparencies, intermediate; *Punctuation and Capitalization*—series of 11 transparencies, primary, intermediate; *Punctuation: Periods, Questions, and Exclamation Marks*—grades 2-5; *Word Usage*—series of 10 transparencies, intermediate, junior high.

29. Laidlaw Brothers, Division of Doubleday; Thatcher and Madison St., River Forest, IL 60305: *Laidlaw Language Experiences Program*—grades K-8; *New Laidlaw Spelling Series*—levels 1-8.

30. Leswing Press, 750 Adrian Way, San Rafael, CA 94903: *Developing Listening Skills*—grades K-6; *Oral Language Skills Series*—grades K-6.

31. Lyon and Carnahan, 407 E. 25 St., Chicago, IL 60616: *Handwriting with Write and See.*

32. McCormick-Mathers Publishing Co., 135 W. 50 St., New York, NY *Skills and Spelling*—levels 1-8.

33. McGraw-Hill Book Co., 1221 Ave. of the Americas, New York, NY 10020: *How to Use an Encyclopedia*—filmstrip.

34. Macmillan Publishing Co., Inc., 866 Third Ave., New York, NY 10022: *Adventures in Handwriting*, plus support materials—grades 1-8; *Composing Language*, English and language arts—grades 1-8; *English Composition*—books 3-8; *Spelling: Sound to Letter*—levels 1-8.

35. Charles E. Merrill Publishing Co., 1300 Alum Creek Dr., Columbus, OH 43216: *Building Reading Power; Merrill Linguistic Readers*—primary grades; *The Productive Thinking Program: A Course in Learning to Think*—upper elementary.

36. Miller-Brody Productions Inc., 342 Madison Ave., New York, NY 10017: *Building Verbal Power I*—records; *Newbery Award Winners*—records; *Sounds for Young Readers*—records.

37. Noble and Noble Publishers, Inc., 1 Dag Hammarskjold Plaza, New York, NY 10017: *Spell/Write*—grades 1-8; *Story-Go-Round*—grades K-3; *Try*—reading readiness experiences, young children.

38. Pacific Production, 414 Mason St., San Francisco, CA 94102: *Learning to Use the Dictionary*—filmstrip.

39. Pied Piper Productions, Box 320, Verdugo City, CA 91046: *English Composition for Children*—series 1, 2, and 3, with filmstrips, teacher's guide, records, cassettes.

40. Popular Science Publishing Co., 355 Lexington Ave., New York, NY 10017: *Goals in Spelling Series*—filmstrip.

41. Prentice-Hall, Englewood Cliffs, NJ 07632: *The Phoenix Reading Series*—grades 4-6; *Spelling Spree*—filmstrips and cassettes.

42. Random House School Division, 201 E. 50 St., New York, NY 10022: *Aware*—poetry learning unit; *Enrichment Records; The Writing Bug*—middle grades.

43. Reader's Digest Services Inc., Education Division, Pleasantville, NY 10570: *Advanced Reading Skills Library; Reading Skill Builder Kits; Reading Skills Library; Reading Tutors; Write to Communicate: The Language Arts in Process*—grades 3-6.

44. Scholastic Magazines and Book Services, 50 W. 44 St., New York, NY 10036: *Creative Expression Series*—five-book writing skills series, grades 2-6; *Firebird Library*—history, biography of minority Americans, grades 5-8; *Scholastic's Listening Skills Program*, units 1, 2—primary, intermediate; *Scholastic's K-3 Poetry Collection; Scholastic's K-6 Pleasure Reading Library.*

45. Science Research Associates, Inc., 155 N. Wacker, Chicago, IL 60611: *Basic Composition Series II and III*—grades 5-8; *Listening Skills Program; Penskill I*—grades 1-3; *Penskill II*—grades 4-6; *Spelling Word Power Laboratory; Words and Patterns; Writing Skills Laboratory.*

46. Scott, Foresman and Co., 1900 E. Lake Ave., Glenview, IL 60025: *Sounds Around Us*—record; *Sounds I Can Hear*—record; *Talkstarters*.

47. Society for Visual Education, Inc., 1345 Diversey Parkway, Chicago, IL 60614: *The Comma Series*—filmstrip; *How to Listen*—filmstrip; *Making English Work for You*—filmstrips, teacher's guide, records, cassettes; *Use Your Library*—filmstrip.

48. Steck-Vaughn Company, Box 2028, Austin, TX 78767: *The Experience Series*; *The Human Values Series*—K-6; *Imaginary Line Handwriting Series*—K-8.

49. Teachers College Press, Columbia University, 1234 Amsterdam Ave., New York, NY 10027: *Composition: Guided-Free*—grades 1-5.

50. Teachers Publishing Corp., Division of Macmillan Publishing, 100 F Brown St., Riverside, NJ 08075: *Listening Games*; *Strengthening Language Skills with Instructional Games*.

51. Troll Associates, 320 Route 17, Mahway, NY 07430: *Listening and Thinking*—intermediate; *New Goals in Listening*—grades 1-3; *New Goals in Listening*—grades 2-4.

52. Webster Division, McGraw-Hill Book Company, 1221 Ave. of the Americas, New York, NY 10020: *English for Today*—grades 2-8; *Learning Language Skills: A Creative Approach*—ages 4-8; *Let's Speak English*—grades 1-6; *Listening Time*—record, grades 1-3; *Programmed Reading*—grades 1-3; *Sullivan Storybooks*—correlated with *Programmed Reading*, grades 1-3; *Tell Again Story Cards*—levels I, II, preschool, grade 1.

53. Xerox Education Publications, 245 Long Hill Rd., Middletown, CT 06457 *Listen! Imagine and Write*—records, books, grades 3-6.

Appendix B

Sources of Free and Inexpensive Teaching Materials

Catalog of Free Teaching Aids; Catalog of Free Teaching Materials. Rubidoux Printing Co., Box 1075, Ventura, CA 93001.

Educators Guide to Free Audio and Video Materials; Educators Guide to Free Films; Educators Guide to Free Filmstrips; Educators Guide to Free Health, Physical, and Recreational Materials; Educators Guide to Free Science Materials; Educators Guide to Free Social Studies Materials; Educators Guide to Free Tapes, Scripts, and Transcripts; Educators Guide to Free Teaching Aids. Educators Progress Service, Inc., 214 Center St., Randolph, WI 53958.

Free and Inexpensive Learning Materials. George Peabody College for Teachers, Division of Surveys and Field Services, Nashville, TN 37203.

Free and Inexpensive Pictures, Pamphlets and Packets for Aerospace Age Education. National Aerospace Educational Council, 806 15 St. N.W., Washington, DC 20005.

Free Learning Materials for Classroom Use. (An annotated list of sources with suggestions for obtaining, evaluating, classifying and using.) The Extension Services, State College of Iowa, Cedar Falls, IA 50613.

List of Materials Available to Secondary School Instructors. B.A. Schuler, Educational Service Bureau, Dow Jones & Co., Inc., Princeton, NJ 98540.

Over 2000 Free Publications, Yours for the Asking. New American Library, Inc., Box 2310, Grand Central Station, New York, NY 10017. (Note: this compilation places substantial reliance upon bulletins, pamphlets, and documents produced by the U.S. Government Printing Office. Rather than actually being free as stated in the title, most cost 5 to 25 cents.)

Selected Free Materials for Classroom Teachers. Fearon Publishers, Inc., 2165 Park Blvd., Palo Alto, CA 94306.

Sources of Free Teaching Aids. Bruce Miller Publications, Box 369, Riverside, CA 92502.

Sources of Teaching Materials. Catherine Williams, Ohio University Press, Columbus, OH 43210.

Other supplemental materials for the classroom are available from such sources as the following:

Bureau of Indian Affairs. U.S. Department of the Interior, 1951 Constitution Ave. N.W., Washington, DC 20242.

Bureau of Mines. U.S. Department of the Interior, 4800 Forbes Ave., Pittsburgh, PA 15213.

Bureau of Reclamation. U.S. Department of the Interior, Washington, DC 20240.

California Redwood Association. 617 Montgomery St., San Francisco, CA 94111.

Forest Service. U.S. Department of Agriculture, Washington, DC 20250.

Fort Ticonderoga Education Services. Box 390, Ticonderoga, NY 12883.

Garden Clubs of America. 598 Madison Ave., New York, NY 10022.

John Hancock Mutual Life Insurance Co. 200 Berkeley St., Boston, MA 02117.

Japan National Tourist Organization. 333 N. Michigan Ave., Chicago, IL 60601.

Pendleton Woolen Mills. Home Economics Department, 218 S.W. Jefferson St., Portland, OR 97201.

Tennessee Valley Authority. Information Office, Knoxville, TN 37902.

U.S. Atomic Energy Commission. Technical Information, Oak Ridge, TN 37830.

Appendix C

Publishers' Addresses

Abelard-Schuman, Ltd.; *see* Intext Press

Abingdon Press, 201 Eighth Ave. S., Nashville, TN 37202

Academic Press, Inc., 111 Fifth Ave., New York, NY 10003

Academic Therapy Publications, 20 Commercial Blvd., Novato, CA 94947

ACL Films, 35 W. 45 St., New York, NY 10036

Acoustifone Corporation, 8954 Comanche Ave., Chatsworth, CA 91311

Adapt Press, 104 E. 20 St., Sioux Falls, SD 57105

Addison-Wesley Publishing Co., Jacob Way, Reading, MA 01867

Allyn and Bacon, Inc., 470 Atlantic Ave., Boston, MA 02210

American Book Co., 135 W. 50 St., New York, NY 10020

American Council on Education, 1 Dupont Circle, N.W. Washington, DC 20036

American Education Publishers, Inc., Education Center, Columbus, OH 43216

American Guidance Service, Inc., Publishers Building, Circle Pines, MN 55014

American Library Association, 50 E. Huron St., Chicago, IL 60611

Amsco School Publications, Inc., 315 Hudson St., New York, NY 10013

Ann Arbor Publishers, Inc., 2057 Charlton Ave., Ann Arbor, MI 48103

Appleton-Century-Crofts; *see* Prentice-Hall, Inc.

Association for Childhood Education International, 3615 Wisconsin Ave.
  N.W. Washington, DC 20016

Association for Instructional Materials, 600 Madison Ave., New York,
  NY 10022

Association for Supervision and Curriculum Development, 225 N. Washington
  St., Alexandria, VA 22314

Atheneum Publishers, 597 Fifth Ave., New York, NY 10017

Audio-Visual Research Company, 1317 Eighth St., S.W., Waseca, MN 56093

Av-Ed Films, 7934 Santa Monica Blvd., Hollywood, CA 90046

Avon Books, 959 Eighth Ave., New York, NY 10019

Bailey Films, Inc., 6509 DeLongpre Ave., Hollywood, CA 90028

Baldridge Reading Instruction Materials, Inc., Box 439, Greenwich, CT 06830

Bantam Books, 666 Fifth Ave., New York, NY 10019

Barnell Loft, Ltd., 958 Church St., Baldwin, NY 11510

Barnhart, Clarence L., Inc., Box 250, Bronxville, NY 10708

Basic Books, Inc., 10 E. 53 St., New York, NY 10022

Beckley-Cardy Company; *see* Benefic Press

Behavioral Research Laboratories, Box 577, Palo Alto, CA 94302

Bell and Howell Co., Audio Visual Products Division, 7100 McCormick Rd., Chicago, IL 60645

Benefic Press, 1250 Sixth Ave., San Diego, CA 92101

Berkley Publishing Corporation; *see* G.P. Putnam's

Better Reading Program, Inc., 230 E. Ohio St., Chicago, IL 60611

BFA Educational Media, 3470 Old Fairburn Rd., Atlanta, GA 30331

Bobbs-Merrill Company, 4300 W. 62 St., Indianapolis, IN 46206

Book Lab Inc., 1449 37 St., Brooklyn, NY 11218

Borg-Warner Educational Systems, 7450 N. Natchez Ave., Niles, IL 60648

Bowker, R. R., Company, 1180 Ave. of the Americas, New York, NY 10036

Bowmar Publishing Company, 622 Rodier Dr., Glendale, CA 91201

Milton Bradley Company, Springfield, MA 01101

Brigham Young University Press, 209 University Press Building, Provo, UT, 84602

Brown University Press, 194 Meeting St., Providence, RI 02912

Brown, Wm. C., Company, 2460 Kerper Blvd., Dubuque, IA 52001

Burgess Publishing Company, 7108 Ohms Lane, Minneapolis, MN 55435

California Association for Neurologically Handicapped Children, Literature Distribution Center, Box 790, Lomita, CA 90717

California Test Bureau/McGraw-Hill, Del Monte Research Park, Monterey, CA 93940

Cambridge Book Company, Inc., Division of New York Times Co., 888 Seventh Ave., New York, NY 10019

Cambridge University Press, 32 E. 57 St., New York, NY 10022

Career Institute, 1500 Cardinal Dr., Little Falls, NJ 07424

Cassettes Unlimited, Roanoke, TX 76262

Cenco Educational Aids, 2600 S. Kostner Ave., Chicago, IL 60623

Center for Applied Linguistics, 1611 N. Kent St., Arlington, VA 22209

Center for Applied Research in Education, Inc., 521 Fifth Ave., New York, NY 10017

Chandler Publishing Company, 124 Spear St., San Francisco, CA 94105

Changing Times Educational Service, 180 E. Fifth St., St. Paul, MN 55101

Childcraft Education Corporation, 150 E. 58 St., New York, NY 10022

Child Study Association of America, Wel-Met, Inc., 50 Madison Ave., New York, NY 10010

Chilton Book Company, Chilton Way, Radnor, PA 19089

Citation Press, 50 W. 44 St., New York, NY 10036

College Skills Center, 1250 Broadway, New York, NY 10001

Committee on Diagnostic Reading Tests, Mountain Home, NC 28758

Communicad, Box 541, Wilton, CT 06897

Consulting Psychologists Press, 577 College Ave., Palo Alto, CA 94306

Continental Press, Inc., 520 E. Bainbridge St., Elizabethtown, PA 17022

Cooperative Tests and Service, Educational Testing Service, Box 999, Princeton, NJ 08504

Coronet Multimedia Co., 65 E. South Water St., Chicago, IL 60601

Coward, McCann and Geoghegan, Inc., 200 Madison Ave., New York, NY 10016

Craig Corporation, 921 W. Artesia Blvd., Compton, CA 90020

Creative Playthings, Box 330, Princeton, NJ 08504

Crestwood House, Box 3427, Highway 66 S., Mankato, MN 56001

Croft Educational Services, 100 Garfield Ave., New London, CT 06320

Crowell, Thomas Y., 521 Fifth Ave., New York, NY 10017

CTB/McGraw-Hill, Del Monte Research Park, Monterey, CA 93940

Cuisenaire Company of America, 9 Elm Ave., Mount Vernon, NY 10550

Curriculum Associates, 94 Bridge St., Chapel Hill Park, Newton, MA 02518

Davco Publishers, 5425 Farao, Skokie, IL 60076

Day, John, Company; *see* Intext Press

Delacorte Press; *see* Dial Press

Dell Publishing Company, 245 E. 47 St., New York, NY 10017

Denoyer Geppert Company, 5325 Ravenswood Ave., Chicago, IL 60640

Department of Health, Education, and Welfare, U.S. Government Printing Office, Washington, DC 20402

Developmental Learning Materials, 7440 Natchez Ave., Niles, IL 60648

Dexter and Westbrook Ltd., 958 Church St., Baldwin, NY 11510

Dial Press, 1 Dag Hammarskjold Plaza, 245 E. 47 St., New York, NY 10017

Dick, A. B., Company, 5700 W. Touhy Ave., Niles, IL 60645

Dickenson Publishing Company, 10 Davis Dr., Belmont, CA 94002

Docent Corporation, 430 Manville Rd., Pleasantville, NY 10570

Dodd, Mead, and Company, Inc., 79 Madison Ave., New York, NY 10016

Doubleday and Company, Inc., 245 Park Ave., New York, NY 10017

Drier Educational Systems, Inc., 255 Fifth Ave., Box 1291, Highland Park, NJ 08904

Dutton, E. P., and Company, 201 Park Ave. S., New York, NY 10002

Early Years Magazine, Box 1223, Darien, Ct 06820

The Economy Company, Box 25308, 1901 N. Walnut St., Oklahoma City, OK 73125

Edmark Associates, 655 I. Orcas St., Seattle, WA 98108

Educational Activities, 1937 Grand Ave., Baldwin, NY 11510

Educational Aids, 845 Wisteria Dr., Fremont, CA 94538

Educational Audio-Visual, Inc., 29 Marble Ave., Pleasantville, NY 10570

Educational Developmental Laboratories, Inc., a Division of McGraw-Hill, 1221 Ave. of the Americas, New York, NY 10036

Educational Games, Box 3653, Grand Central Station, New York, NY 10017

Educational and Industrial Testing Service, Box 7234, San Diego, CA 92107

Educational Press Association of America, Glassboro State College, Glassboro, NJ 08028

Educational Progress, Box 45663, Tulsa, OK 74145

Educational Records Bureau, 3 E. 80 St., New York, NY 10021

Educational Service, Inc., Box 219, Stevensville, MI 49127

Educational Teaching Aids, 159 W. Kinzie St., Chicago, IL 60610

Educational Testing Service, Princeton, NJ 08540

Educators Publishing Service, 75 Moulton St., Cambridge, MA 02138

EMC Corporation, 180 E. Sixth St., St. Paul, MN 55101

Encyclopaedia Britannica Educational Corporation, 425 N. Michigan Ave., Chicago, IL 60611

ERIC Clearinghouse on Reading and Communications Skills, 1111 Kenyon Rd., Urbana, IL 61801

ERIC Clearinghouse on Tests, Educational Testing Service, Princeton, NJ 08540

Essay Press, Box 5, Planetarium Station, New York, NY 10024

Exceptional Products Corporation, Box 6404, Richfield Branch, Minneapolis, MN 55423

Exposition Press, Inc., 900 S. Oyster Bay Rd., Hicksville, NY 11801

Eye Gate House, Inc., 146–01 Archer Ave., Jamaica, NY 11435

Fawcett Book Group, 1515 Broadway, New York, NY 10036

Fearon-Pitman Publishers, 6 Davis Dr., Belmont, CA 94002

Field Educational Publications, Inc., 609 Mission St., San Francisco, CA 94105

Follett Publishing Company, 1010 W. Washington Blvd., Chicago, IL 60607

Four Winds Press, 50 W. 44 St., New York, NY 10036

Free Press; *see* Macmillan Publishing Company

Funk and Wagnalls, Inc., 53E. 57 St., New York, NY 10021

Gable Academies, 770 Miller Rd., Miami, FL 33155

Garrard Publishing Company, 1607 N. Market St., Champaign, IL 61820

General Learning Corporation, 250 James St., Morristown, NJ 07960

Gillingham-Slingerland Reading Workshops, 75 Moulton St., Cambridge, MA 02138

Ginn and Company, 191 Spring St., Lexington, MA 02173

Globe Book Company, 50 W. 23 St., New York, NY 10010

Golden Gate Junior Books, a Division of Children's Press, 1224 W. Van Buren St., Chicago, IL 60607

Golden Press; *see* Western Publishing Company

Goodyear Publishing, 1640 Fifth St., Santa Monica, CA 90401

The Grade Teacher, Riverside, NJ 08075

Grolier Educational Corporation, Sherman Turnpike, Danbury CT 06816

Grossett and Dunlap, 51 Madison Ave., New York, NY 10010

Grune and Stratton, Inc., *see* Academic Press, Inc.

Gryphon Press, 220 Montgomery St., Highland Park, NJ 08904

Hammond, Inc., 515 Valley St., Maplewood, NJ 07040

Harcourt Brace Jovanovich, 757 Third Ave., New York, NY 10017

Harper and Row, Inc., 10 E. 53 St., New York, NY 10022

Harr-Wagner; *see* Field Educational Publications

Harvard University Press, 79 Garden St., Cambridge, MA 02138

Harvey House, 20 Waterside Plaza, New York, NY 10010

Hastings House, Inc., 10 E. 40 St., New York, NY 10016

Heath, D.C., and Company, 125 Spring St., Lexington, MA 02173

Highlights for Children, 803 Church St., Honesdale, PA 18431

Hoffman Information Systems, 4423 Arden Dr., El Monte, CA 91734

Holiday House, Inc., 18 E. 53 St., New York, NY 10022

Holt, Rinehart and Winston, Inc., 383 Madison Ave., New York, NY 10017

Horn Book, Inc., Park Square Building, 31 St. James Ave., Boston, MA 02116

Houghton Mifflin Company, 1 Beacon St., Boston, MA 02107

Ideal School Supply Company, 11000 S. Lavergne Ave., Oak Lawn, IL 60453

Imperial International Learning Corporation, Box 548, Kankakee, IL 60901

Individualized Instruction Inc., Box 25308, Oklahoma City, OK 73125

Initial Teaching Alphabet Publications, 6 E. 43 St., New York, NY 10017

Innovations for Individualizing Instruction, Box 4361, Washington, DC 20402

Instructional Communications Technology, Inc., 10 Stepar Place, Huntington Station, New York, NY 11743

Instructional Fair, 4158 Lake Michigan Dr., Grand Rapids, MI 49504

Instructional Objectives Exchange, 10884 Santa Monica Blvd., Los Angeles, CA 90025

The Instructo Corporation, Cedar Hollow and Matthews Road, Paoli, PA 19301

Instructor Publications, 7 Bank St., Dansville, NY 14437

International Film Bureau, 332 S. Michigan Ave., Chicago, IL 60604

International Reading Association, 800 Barksdale Rd., Newark, DE 19711

Intext Press, 257 Park Ave. S., New York, NY 10010

Jamestown Publishers, Box 6743, Providence, RI 02940

Johns Hopkins University Press, Baltimore, MD 21218

Jones, Charles A., Publishing Company, a Division of Wadsworth Publishing Co., Inc., 4 Village Green, Worthington, OH 43085

Jones-Kenilworth Co., 8801 Ambassador Dr., Dallas TX 75247

Judy Publishing Company, Box 5270, Chicago, IL 60608

Kendall/Hunt Publishing Company, 2460 Kerper Blvd., Dubuque, IA 52001

Kenworthy Educational Service, Inc., Box 60, Buffalo, NY 14205

Keystone View Co., 2212 E. 12 St., Davenport, IA 52803

Kingsbury; *see* Remedial Education Press

Klamath Printing Company, 320 Lowell St., Klamath Falls, OR 97601

Knopf, Alfred A., a Subsidiary of Random House, Inc., 201 E. 50 St., New York, NY 10022

Laidlaw Bros., a Division of Doubleday and Company, Thatcher and Madison, River Forest, IL 60305

Language Research Associates, 175 E. Delaware Place, Chicago, IL 60611

Learn, Inc., 113 Gaither Dr., Mount Laurel, NJ 08054

Learning Corporation of America, 711 Fifth Ave., New York, NY 10022

Learning Materials, Inc., 100 E. Ohio St., Chicago, IL 60611

Learning Research Associates, 1501 Broadway, New York, NY 10036

Learning Through Seeing, Inc., Box 268, LTS Building, Sunland, CA 91040

Lerner Publication Company, 241 First Ave. N., Minneapolis, MN 55401

Leswing Press, Inc., 750 Adrian Way, San Rafael, CA 94903

Let's Read, Box 250, Bronxville, NY 10466

Lippincott, J. B., Company, E. Washington Square, Philadelphia, PA 19105

Little, Brown and Company, 34 Beacon St., Boston, MA 02106

Lothrop, Lee and Shepard Books, 105 Madison Ave., New York, NY 10016

Love Publishing Company, 6635 E. Villanova Place, Denver, CO 80222

McCormick-Mathers Publishing Co., 135 W. 50 St., New York, NY 10020

McGraw-Hill Book Company, 1221 Ave. of the Americas, New York, NY 10020

McKay, David, Company, Inc., 2 Park Ave., New York, NY 10016

Macmillan Publishing Company, 866 Third Ave., New York, NY 10022

Macrae Smith Company, Rte. 54 and Old 147, Turbotville, PA 17772

Mafex Associates, 90 Cherry St., Johnstown, PA 15902

Maico Hearing Instruments, 7375 Bush Lake Rd., Minneapolis, MN 55435

Marie's Educational Materials, 195 S. Murphy Ave., Sunnyvale, CA 94086

Mast-Keystone, 2212 E. 12 St., Davenport, IA 52803

Melmont Publishers, 1224 W. Van Buren, Chicago, IL 60607

Meredith Corporation, 1716 Locust St., Des Moines, IA 50336

Merrill, Charles E., Publishing Company, 1300 Alum Creek Dr., Columbus, OH 43216

Messner, Julian, Inc., 1230 Ave. of the Americas, New York, NY 10020

Michigan State University Press, 1405 S. Harrison Rd., East Lansing, MI 48824

Milliken Publishing Company, Sound Photo Equipment, Box 2953, Lubbock, TX 97408

The Mills Center, Inc., 1512 E. Broward Blvd., Fort Lauderdale, FL 33301

Milton Bradley, Springfield, MA 01001

MIT Press, 28 Carleton St., Cambridge, MA 02142

MKM Inc., 809 Kansas City St., Rapid City, SD 57701

Modern Curriculum Press, Inc., 13900 Prospect Rd., Cleveland, OH 44136

Morrow, William, and Company, 105 Madison Ave., New York, NY 10016

Mosby, C.V., Company, 11830 Westline Industrial Dr., St. Louis, MO 63141

National Assessment Office, Rm 201A, Huron Towers, 222 Fuller Rd., Ann Arbor, MI 48105

National Association of the Deaf, 814 Thayer Ave., Silver Spring, MD 20910

National Council of Teachers of English, 1111 Kenyon Rd., Urbana, IL 61801

Nelson, Thomas, and Sons, Ltd., 36 Park St., London WIY, England

Nelson, Thomas, Inc., 405 Seventh Ave. S., Nashville, TN 37203

New Century; *see* Meredith Corporation

New Dimensions in Education, 925 Westchester Ave., White Plains, NY 10604

New Readers Press, Box 131, Syracuse, NY 13210

Noble and Noble Publishers, 1 Dag Hammarskjold Plaza, New York, NY 10017

Odyssey Press, Ltd., 4300 W. 62 St., Indianapolis, IN 46206

Ohio State University Press, Hitchcock Hall, Rm. 316, 2070 Neil Ave., Columbus, OH 43210

Open Court Publishing Company, 1058 Eighth St., LaSalle, IL 61301

The Orton Society, Inc., 8415 Bellona Lane, Suite 204, Towson, MD 21204

Owen, F. A., Publishing Co., 7 Bank St., Dansville, NY 14437

Oxford University Press, 200 Madison Ave., New York, NY 10016

Pacifica Foundation, Pacifica Tape Library, Department E, 5316 Venice Blvd., Los Angeles, CA 90019

Parents Magazine Press, 52 Vanderbilt Ave., New York, NY 10017

Parker Publishing Company, *see* Prentice-Hall, Inc.

Peabody, George, College for Teachers, Nashville, TN 37203

Peacock, F. E., Publishers, 401 W. Irving Park Rd., Itasca, IL 60143

Pendulum Press, Inc., Saw Mill Rd., West Haven, CT 06516

Penguin Books, Inc., 625 Madison Ave., New York, NY 10022

Perceptual Development Laboratories, Box 1911, Big Springs, TX 79720

Personnel Press, 191 Spring St., Lexington, MA 02173

Phonovisual Products, 12216 Parklawn Dr., Rockville, MD 20852

Plays Inc., 8 Arlington St., Boston, MA 02116

Playskool, Division of Milton Bradley, Springfield, MA 01101

Popular Library, Unit of CBS, 1515 Broadway, New York, NY 10036

Prentice-Hall, Inc., Englewood Cliffs, NJ 07632

The Psychological Corporation; *see* Harcourt Brace Jovanovich

Psychological Test Specialists, Box 1441, Missoula, MT 59801

Psychotechnics, Inc., 1900 Pickwick Ave., Glenview, IL 60025

Purdue University Audio-Visual Center, Lafayette, IN 47901

Putnam's, G. P., Sons, 200 Madison Ave., New York, NY 10016

Pyramid Books, 919 Third Ave., New York, NY 10022

Random House, 201 E. 50 St., New York, NY 10022

Reader's Choice, Division of Scholastic Magazines, 50 W. 44 St., New
York, NY 10036

Reader's Digest, Educational Division, Pleasantville, NY 10570

The Reading Institute of Boston, 116 Newbury St., Boston, MA 02116

Reading Is Fun-Damental, Smithsonian Institute, Washington, DC 20560

The Reading Laboratory, Inc., 55 Day St., South Norwalk, CT 06854

Reading Newsreport, 11 W. 42 St., New York, NY 10026

Remedial Education Press, Kingsbury Center, 2138 Bancroft Place N.W.,
Washington, DC 20008

Right to Read, 400 Maryland Ave. S.W., Washington, DC 20202

The Ronald Press Company, 605 Third Ave., New York, NY 10016

Sadlier, William H., 11 Park Place, New York, NY 10007

Saunders, W. B., Company, W. Washington Square, Philadelphia, PA 19105

Scarecrow Press, Inc., 52 Liberty St., Box 656, Metuchen, NJ 08840

Scholastic Magazines and Book Services, 50 W. 44 St., New York, NY 10036

Scholastic Test Service, Inc., Bensenville, IL 60106

Science Research Associates, Inc., 155 N. Wacker Dr., Chicago, IL 60606

Scott, Foresman and Company, 1900 E. Lake Ave., Glenview, IL 60025

Scott, William R., Inc., 333 Sixth Ave., New York, NY 10014

Scribner's, Charles, Sons, 597 Fifth Ave., New York, NY 10017

The Seabury Press, 815 Second Ave., New York, NY 10017

Selected Academic Readings, 630 Fifth Ave., New York, NY 10017

Silver Burdett Division, General Learning Corporation, 250 James St., Morristown, NJ 07960

Simon and Schuster, Inc., 1230 Ave. of the Americas, New York, NY 10020

Singer Co., Graflex Division, 3750 Monroe Ave., Rochester, NY 14603

Singer Education and Training Products, Society for Visual Education,
1345 Diversey Parkway, Chicago, IL 60614

Singer, L. W., Inc., a Division of Random House, 201 E. 50 St., New York,
NY 10022

Skill Development Equipment Company, a Division of Port-a-Pit, 1340 N. Jefferson, Anaheim, CA 92806

Slosson Educational Publications, 140 Pine St., East Aurora, NY 14052

Society for Visual Education, Inc., 1345 Diversey Parkway, Chicago, IL 60614

Special Child Publications, 4635 Union Bay Place, N.E. Seattle, WA 98105

Spellbinder, 33 Bradford St., Concord, MA 01743

Spoken Arts, Inc., 310 N. Ave., New Rochelle, NY 10801

Stanwix House, 3020 Chartiers Ave., Pittsburgh, PA 15204

Steck-Vaughn Company, Box 2028, Austin, TX 78768

Steolting Co., 1350 S. Kostner Ave., Chicago, IL 60623

Superintendent of Documents, U.S. Government Printing Office, Washington, DC 20402

Syracuse University Press, 1011 E. Water St., Syracuse, NY 13210

Teachers College Press, Columbia University, 1234 Amsterdam Ave., New York, NY 10027

Teachers Publishing, a Division of Macmillan Publishing Co., Inc., 100 F Brown St., Riverside, NJ 08075

Teaching Resources Corporation, 100 Boylston St., Boston, MA 02116

Teaching Technology Corporation, 2103 Green Spring Dr., Timonium, MD 21093

Thomas, Charles C., Publisher, 301-27 E. Lawrence Ave., Springfield, IL 62717

Titmus Optical Vision Testers, 1312 W. 7 St., Piscataway, NJ 08854

Trend Enterprises, Box 3073, St. Paul, MN 55163

University of Chicago Press, 5801 S. Ellis Ave., Chicago, IL 60637

University of Illinois Press, 54 E. Gregory Dr., Champaign, IL 61820

University of Iowa, Bureau of Audio-Visual Instruction, Iowa City, IA 52240

University of Minnesota Press, 2037 University Ave., S.E., Minneapolis, MN 55455

University Park Press, 233 E. Redwood St., Baltimore, MD 21202

Vanguard Press, Inc., 424 Madison Ave., New York, NY 10017

Van Nostrand Reinhold, 135 W. 50 St., New York, NY 10020

Van Wagenen Psychological Educational Laboratories, 1729 Irvin Ave. S., Minneapolis, MN 55403

Viking Press, Inc., 625 Madison Ave., New York, NY 10022

Wadsworth, 10 Davis Dr., Belmont, CA 94002

Walck, Henry Z., Inc., 2 Park Ave., New York, NY 10016

Warne, Frederick, and Company, 2 Park Ave., New York, NY 10016

Washington Square Press, Inc., 1230 Ave. of the Americas, New York, NY 10020

Watts, Franklin, Inc., 730 Fifth Ave., New York, NY 10019

Wayne State University Press, 5959 Woodward Ave., Detroit, MI 48202

Webster, a Division of McGraw-Hill Book Company, 1221 Ave. of the Americas, New York, NY 10020

Weekly Reader, 245 Longhill Rd., Middletown, CT 06457

Western Psychological Services, 12031 Wilshire Blvd., Los Angeles, CA 90025

Western Publishing Company, 850 Third Ave., New York, NY 10022

Westinghouse Learning Corporation, 5005 W. 110 St., Oak Lawn, IL 60453

Whitman, Albert, and Company, 560 W. Lake St., Chicago, IL 60606

Wiley, John, and Sons, Inc., 605 Third Ave., New York, NY 10016

Williams and Wilkins Company, 428 E. Preston St., Baltimore, MD 21202

Wilson, H. W., Company, 950 University Ave., Bronx, NY 10452

Winston Press, 430 Oak Grove, Minneapolis, MN 55403

Winter Haven Lions Research Foundation, Inc., Box 112, Winter Haven, FL 33880

Wisconsin Design for Reading Skill, Interpretive Scoring Systems, 4401 W. 76 St., Minneapolis, MN 55435

Wisconsin Research and Development Center for Cognitive Learning, Madison, WI 53706

Word Games, Box 305, Healdsburg, CA 95448

Workshop Center for Open Education, 6 Shepherd Hall, City College of New York, Convent Ave. and 140 St., New York, NY 10031

World Publishing Company, 280 Park Ave., New York, NY 10017

Xerox Education Publications, 245 Long Hill Rd., Middletown, CT 06457

Young Readers Press; *see* Simon and Schuster, Inc.

Zaner-Bloser Company, 612 N. Park St., Columbus, OH 43215

Zweig, Richard L., Associates, 20800 Beach Blvd., Huntington Beach, CA 92648

Subject-Skill Index of Activities

Notes

Notes

Notes

Notes

Notes

Notes

Notes

Notes

Notes

Notes

Student Response Form

We would appreciate having your reactions to *Language Arts Activities for Elementary Schools.* Your comments and suggestions will help us to respond to the needs of users of future editions. Please complete this questionnaire and return it to College Marketing, Houghton Mifflin Company, One Beacon Street, Boston, MA 02107.

1. Do you like the format of the book? Yes _____ No _____

2. Do you like the organization of the book? Yes _____ No _____

3. What material and features did you find most useful? _____

   _____

   _____

4. Which material or features were least useful? Why? _____

   _____

   _____

5. We would like to know your reaction to coverage provided by the activities. Please indicate whether too many or too few activities were presented for the topics listed.

	Too many activities	Too few activities
a. Language study	_____	_____
b. Grammar	_____	_____
c. Pre/early school language arts	_____	_____
d. Listening	_____	_____
e. Oral composition	_____	_____
f. Written composition	_____	_____
g. Spelling	_____	_____
h. Handwriting	_____	_____
i. Vocabulary development	_____	_____
j. Appreciation/uses of language	_____	_____
k. Language arts within content areas	_____	_____

6. Did you find the directions for activities clear and easy to understand? Yes _____ No _____

   If not, cite activity number(s) _____

   _____

7. Did the introductions to the chapters meet your needs? Yes _____ No _____

   If not, what is lacking _____

   _____

8. Does the subject-skill index meet your needs? Yes _____ No _____

   If not, what is lacking? _____

   _____

   _____

9. We welcome any additional comments you would care to make. _____

   _____

   _____

   _____